Walks in the
Slow Lanes of
ESSEX

© Angie Jones, 2021

All Rights Reserved. No part of this publication may be reproduced, stored in a retrieval system, or transmitted in any form or by any means – electronic, mechanical, photocopying, recording, or otherwise – without prior written permission from the publisher or a licence permitting restricted copying issued by the Copyright Licensing Agency, 90 Tottenham Court Road, London W1P 0LA. This book may not be lent, resold, hired out or otherwise disposed of by trade in any form of binding or cover other than that in which it is published, without the prior consent of the publisher.

Moral Rights: The author has asserted her moral right to be identified as the Author of this Work.

Published by Sigma Leisure – an imprint of
Sigma Press, Stobart House, Pontyclerc, Penybanc Road, Ammanford, Carmarthenshire SA18 3HP.

British Library Cataloguing in Publication Data
A CIP record for this book is available from the British Library.

ISBN: 978-1-910758-49-6

Typesetting and Design by: Sigma Press, Ammanford.

Cover: © Angie Jones

Photographs: © Angie Jones

Maps: © Angie Jones

Printed by: Akcent Media

Disclaimer: the information in this book is given in good faith and is believed to be correct at the time of publication. No responsibility is accepted by either the author or publisher for errors or omissions, or for any loss or injury however caused. Only you can judge your own fitness, competence and experience. Do not rely solely on sketch maps for navigation: we strongly recommend the use of appropriate Ordnance Survey (or equivalent) maps.

Walks in The Slow Lanes of Essex

Angie Jones

This book is dedicated to my two little grandsons, Eli and Ethan, who perhaps one day, when they are bigger, will walk in my footsteps.

Acknowledgement

My heartfelt thanks to God for giving me a husband who has graciously shared every moment of this adventure.

Contents

Location of Walks   6

Introduction   9

The Walks
1. Castle Hedingham   11
2. Lamarsh   19
3. Great Sampford   26
4. Foxearth   33
5. Navestock   40
6. Great and Little Henny   46
7. Terling   53
8. Matching Tye   60
9. Stock   67
10. Blackmore End   74
11. High Roding to Great Canfield   81
12. Stisted   88
13. Tollesbury   96
14. West Hanningfield   103
15. Coggeshall   110
16. Great and Little Maplestead   117
17. Wrabness   124
18. Little Easton   131
19. Pleshey   138

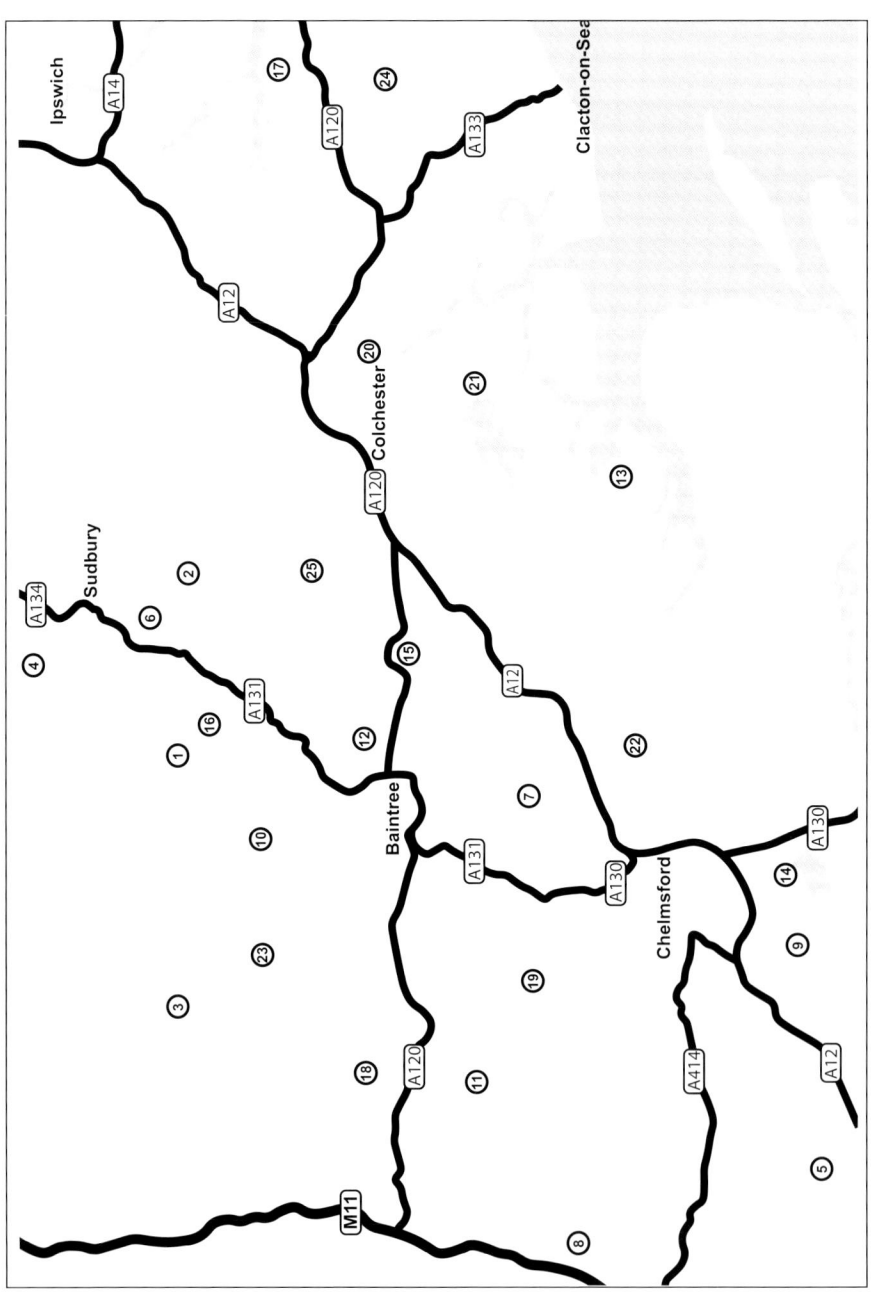

20. Greenstead Green	146
21. Abberton	153
22. Ulting	160
23. Great Bardfield	168
24. Beaumont Cum Moze	176
25. Chappel and Wakes Colne	184

Introduction

Essex. My home county. I thought I knew it well but in writing this book I have found a rich tapestry of landscapes, from salty creeks and stunning scenery, to quiet villages shaped by their past.

It has been a joy to explore Essex and this book invites you to come with me on twenty five walks, none too demanding, taking time to linger and learn along the way; to discover the secrets they harbour.

I have written for people who enjoy delving into the hidden history of the places we visit; to notice and enjoy the beauty of the flowers and hedgerows and to hear some stories about local characters.

Essex offers tiny hamlets of picturesque cottages against a backdrop of far-reaching fields, a railway museum and a nature reserve or two; mills, churches and castles; shimmering estuaries; windswept salt marshes, shadowy woodlands and we even stumble over a forgotten lime kiln.

And believe it - Essex is NOT flat! There are some steep roads that rise then fall to lonely farms nestling deep in pretty valleys.

Each walk includes a comfort stop at a local café or pub, but with the Covid cloud of uncertainty currently threatening our hospitality industry, I've added contact details to enable you to check opening times and service offered BEFORE your visit, to avoid disappointment.

Perhaps taking a picnic these days is a safer option? Look out for suggestions of good places to munch your sandwiches with an old-fashioned flask of tea.

As in my book (*Walks in the Slow Lanes of Suffolk*), my husband, Maurice (Mogs) appears in some of the photos. For a bit of fun, see if you can spot him?

The need at this time, to escape into, and absorb the beauty of the created world around us is even more crucial for our bodies and our souls. Please join me as we walk together in the slow lanes of Essex.

Angie Jones

Walk 1: Castle Hedingham

Nestled in the Colne Valley is the village of Castle Hedingham, watched over by a mighty Norman Keep that commands views of the surrounding countryside.

It is just the place for an afternoon walk and I park my car in St James' Street outside the village shop where I can buy take-away coffee and tempting cakes from a local bakery either at the start or end of my walk (or perhaps both)! I promptly decide that this will be my starting and finishing place, or I could enjoy a cream tea in The Tea Shop at the Old Moothouse, but first I must work up an appetite!

This easy walk takes you through the village and on a circular route around the castle grounds but in places it is quite steep. It skirts fields and crosses pastureland, where sheep may be grazing. There are no stiles, only romantic kissing gates!

Distance	Almost 2 miles or 3.0 km
Time	1½ hours
Start	Find a space in the village streets or use the car park behind the Memorial Hall in Castle Lane (no charge)
Terrain	Steep in places
Map	OS Explorer 195 Braintree & Saffron Walden
Refreshments	The Tea Shop at the Moot House 01787 460342 sarah@moothouserestaurant.co.uk Tuesday - Sunday; 9.30am - 4.00pm. Homemade cakes! The Bell, 01787 460350 and The Wheatsheaf, 01787 460 769. also serve food. The Village shop sells sandwiches, cakes and hot drinks. There are several benches on route where a picnic could be enjoyed.
Toilets	Public toilets behind the Memorial Hall, a red-bricked building which is close to the churchyard

Getting there	By car take the A1017 in Sible Hedingham or take the B1058 from Sudbury. Bus. No. 89 Hedingham Buses run every hour from Braintree to Great Yeldham stopping near The Bell

1. Stand facing The Bell in St James' Street outside the village shop and turn left to walk past Bank House (on your left). There is a blue plaque attached to the red bricks. Eric Ravillious, an artist renowned for his woodcarvings and book illustrations, lived there until 1942. He was an official war artist, an honorary captain in the Royal Marines, but on a sea mission over Iceland, his plane failed to return.

2. Soon you come to an ancient herringbone wall with some Roman bricks where pigeons constantly attack the old lime mortar. Here is the tennis club. Across the road is 'Spencers' with a bay window that betrays its past as a shoemaker's shop. Here Joseph Jay and five generations of his family made shoes from the 1700s.

3. As you reach the end of St James' Street you will see a red brick house (number 37) which was once a pottery, and this reminds me that Edward Bingham, a potter, once lived and worked here too. This little patch of grass is Forge Green. Here horses waited to be shod or pilgrims gathered before they crossed the road to take the waters from St James' Well which today is marked by an unassuming brick building that serves as a pump house to the bore hole beneath.

4. To your left is Bayley Street which leads to the gate of Hedingham Castle, but this walk takes you *around* its boundaries, so go up Sudbury Hill. The former playing field across the road was the site of a hospital built around 1250, but there are no give-away signs today, neither any evidence of St James' chapel which was a ruin in 1678.

5. Go up the hill until you see concrete steps on the other side of the road. Here is our detour- to the spot where a windmill once stood. It was demolished in 1878. There is no trace of the mill but walk to the corner of the field, passing steep gardens on your right, to enjoy wonderful views of the lovely countryside.

6. Retrace your steps back down the hill and near the 40 mph sign, you find a pathway which climbs steeply between chestnut-paling fence and a

tangle of brambles and undergrowth. Here and there on your left you can catch glimpses of the castle lakes.

There is a sad, local story of Poll Miles, thought to be a witch, because animals seemed to be drawn to her. It is said that she drowned herself in the lake at the castle in 1912 and is buried at a crossroads nearby – considered unworthy of hallowed ground. I think of her as I climb the narrow path, littered with pine cones and my legs begin to ache.

7. To your left you can see the Norman Keep towering above the trees. William the Conqueror gave The Hedinghams to the De Veres in 1086 and the castle was built in 1140 by Aubrey de Vere. The square keep with its 3.4 metre thick walls has survived the centuries, despite two sieges in 1216 and 1217. It boasts the biggest Norman arch in Europe and is approached by a Tudor bridge spanning a dry moat. Through the trees look for the dovecote, built in 1720.

The Norman Keep

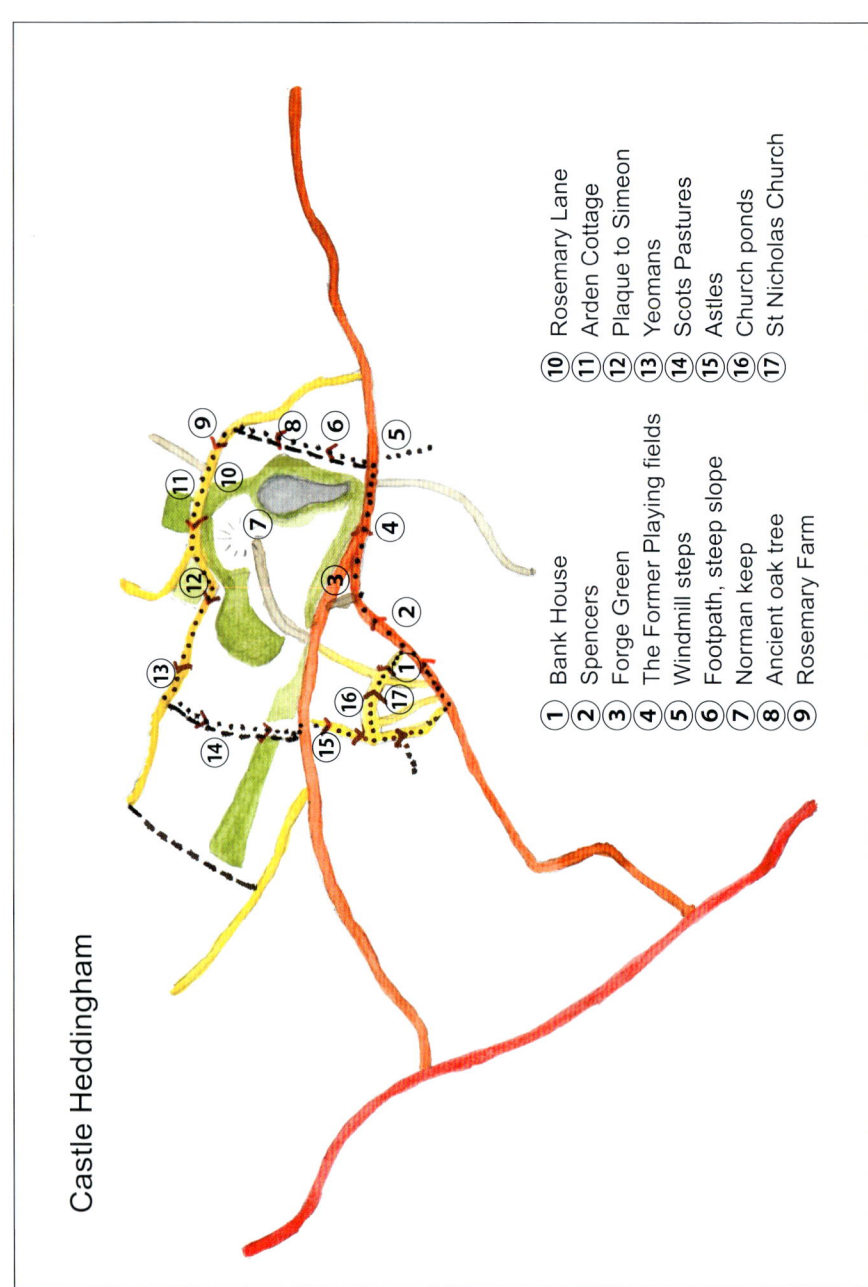

8. The path (thankfully) levels out and you pass an ancient oak tree with deeply ridged bark on the massive trunk. Pause to look up at its mighty branches.

The walking is easier now and to my right are some old iron railings entwined and in some places engulfed by a hedgerow. Then suddenly I am in an open space with a cornfield stretching away to my left. Here, in the autumn there are juicy blackberries waiting to be harvested and made into jam. I feel like Moses parting the waves of the Red Sea as I walk between the fields with the wind rippling the dark green wheat stalks.

Footpath to Rosemary Farm

9. Go across the field towards Rosemary Farm and as you reach the bank to the lane note the remains of a brick wall almost hidden by grass and moss. Once there stood a Nissan hut here which it is said housed a search light during the Second World War.

10. Now you are in Rushley Green where I have lived for many years. Turn left by a big horse chestnut tree whose sticky buds I cannot resist touching in early spring. The big barn has an interesting weather vane on it – a gift to the owner on his 80th birthday from all the neighbours, commemorating his renowned home-made wine!

11. Continue along the road that passes through a woodland of ivy clad trees, whose floor is littered with fallen branches. At the fork bear left into an avenue of towering lime trees planted in 1879. This is 'Lady Margaret's Walk' named after Lady Majendie whose family owned Hedingham Castle for 250 years.

12. On the right is Rushley Green with benches if you need to rest and a plaque to my son, Simeon Jones who lived here until his sudden death from a heart attack, at the age of fifteen.

Keeper's Cottage

Protestant preachers used this spot to proclaim their faith during the 18th and 19th centuries.

Ahead there is thatched 'Keepers Cottage' – a gamekeeper perhaps, who worked at the Castle? The lane curves round to the right. In the spring there are snowdrops and pale primroses in the verges.

13. The next building, behind a picket fence entwined with sweetly-scented, old roses, is another medieval house; 'Yeomans' and opposite this is a farm gate and a lovely view of gentle meadow-land that drops away down into woodland. This is the next part of your journey. Go through the kissing gate.

14. *Beyond the kissing gate is Scot's Pasture where sheep graze and in winter well wrapped-up village children come dragging their sledges as soon as the first snowflake falls. From this spot you would never know that the village of Castle Hedingham lies hidden below amongst the trees in the valley. I walk down the meadow with castle land on my left where in May I can see a carpet of bluebells and catch their fragrance as I pass. On the*

right is another huge oak tree with mysterious dark burrows disappearing beneath its roots.

At the bottom of the pasture a kissing gate takes you to a well-worn path.

The field on your right was once the scene of jousting tournaments and if you pause and let your imagination run wild you can picture foam-flecked horses and hear their hooves thundering on the turf.

Follow the uneven path until you pass housing estate, Bowman's Park (right) whose name gives us a clue to its past. Soon you come to Pye Corner.

15. Before you is 'Astles', a rambling 18th century red brick house which was once an inn, where De Vere Stackpoole wrote *The Blue Lagoon*. Here is a row of pretty cottages and one is called 'Straw Platters'. There were many cottage industries in the village, and weaving and straw plaiting were among them. Brick making and farming were the main employers.

Cross the road and walk down Crown Street and see an intriguing arched wooden door in a high wall, which reminds me of 'The Secret Garden' and I wonder what lies on the other side?

Church Ponds

16. There is evidence of other shops here – with their 'give-away' windows. Number 5 was once a butcher's and opposite it stood a greengrocer both sadly closed in recent years. Bear left into Church Ponds. (Church lane takes you to the Memorial Hall and public toilets.)

Look out for 'The Old Bakery' and 'Melford' (once a barber's shop). You will find yourself in Falcon Square with timber-framed 'Falcon House' where a

Falcon Square

mullet (star) is carved on a beam; a sign of the De Veres. This too was an inn and behind its wide wooden gateway is a green lane used by the falconer as a direct link to the castle. Bear right into King Street or take a diversion to visit the ancient church of St Nicholas.

17. *Once a Saxon church stood on this site, and a Saxon stone can be seen in the South Chapel. There are three original Norman doors and as I step inside I see the huge Norman arches; the hammer-beam roof and the Wheel Window, one of only five remaining in England. As I explore, I find a cold, stone tomb with a figure of John de Vere and his countess carved on it. Outside again there are more signs of this family, with boars and mullets – their heraldic symbols.*

18. Now you are back to the starting place St James' Street. Look for the 15th century 'Moot House' – now a restaurant and tea shop and 'The Bell', a 16th century Inn where stage coaches once stopped on their way to London. (There is a milestone outside.)

    And now I am back to my starting place and the village shop, so its decision time. Shall I have an iced bun or a jam doughnut or take a few steps to the nearby Tea Shop for a cream tea?

Celebration in Castle Hedingham

Walk 2: Lamarsh

Just a stone's throw from Suffolk, overlooking the river Stour, amidst lovely countryside sits the little village of Lamarsh. This is a circular walk that rises and falls with the gently rolling landscape. Follow country lanes, pass through wild flower meadows and skirt woodland and edges of fields.

Distance	2.4 miles or 4km
Time	1½ hours
Start	Roadside parking near the centre of the village
Terrain	Up or down all the way!
Map	OS Explorer 196 Sudbury, Hadleigh & Dedham Vale
Refreshments	The Henny Swan is two miles from Sudbury, 01787 267953 hennyswan@gmail.com Wickham St Paul: The Victory Inn at The Ship 01787 269364
Toilets	No public loos in Lamarsh
Getting there	From Sudbury take the A131 to Halstead and turn left towards Bures at the bottom of Ballingdon Hill. Follow this narrow lane as it twists and turns past Middleton and Henny Street with the river Stour on your left and gentle hills rising on your right. (Alternatively from Bures take the road to Lamarsh.) There is no bus service

1. Drive past the round tower of Lamarsh church on your left and look for a place to park by the road side. You are entering the tiny village.

   This is just what I did on a beautiful blue-sky morning in early spring. I left my car near the telephone box, by Brook bungalows and turned right towards the houses.

Church and view, Lamarsh

Reynolds, Lamarsh

Orchard House, Lamarsh

2. At Brook House, the home of a brewer and beer seller in the 17th century, turn right towards Alphamstone where you will see a lovely old thatched house – Reynolds on the corner. This is Lamarsh Road and you will find that it is lined with a pleasing mix of old and new properties.

I came to Holly Cottage where daffodils peeped over a low brick wall and everywhere white narcissi seemed to overflow from gardens. I saw April Cottage has a thick thatch then Orchard House appeared on my left, a fine medieval hall with an elaborate brick chimney stack. It was once called Street Farm.

3. Keep on the road until you see a footpath sign pointing left, by a new bungalow. It follows the course of the stream with its soothing gurgle of flowing water. The path leads to open pasture land. Keep the hedge to your left.

From the trees on my left came the whining roar of a chainsaw and the smell of petrol. Hazel catkins hung from thin branches where great tits called – their repetitive notes reminding me of someone pumping up a bicycle tyre.

4. You will see newly planted woodland with young saplings, then take the right path up the hillside where brambles arch over rough grassland and brash yellow splashes of dandelions flower in spring and summer. As you ascend, faraway views of Suffolk will become visible between the trees, and look out for the tiny train chugging across the Stour valley. The railway was built in 1848, when mammoth tusks were found during its construction. It once connected Colchester and Cambridge, but now carries passengers from Sudbury to Marks Tey passing through lovely countryside and over Chappel viaduct.

5. With Parkhill Wood and its bluebells and yellow stars of celandine in spring on your left, continue straight along the path which falls down to another stream where a concrete pipe serves as a bridge. Look for an information board just after you've crossed the stream.

A sign told me there is permissive access to a wild flower meadow and to the right – the site of a roman villa. As I tramped up the slope where last year's knapweed created a brown haze of seed-heads, I noticed young green leaves of cow mumble, plaintain and buttercups giving hints of the beauty to come.

6. Across the field you will soon see the red-tiled roof and wooden tower of St Barnabas Church. The path curves right along the field edge to take you towards it. Soon you will reach the road where you cross by a telephone box.

St Barnabas Church, Alphamstone

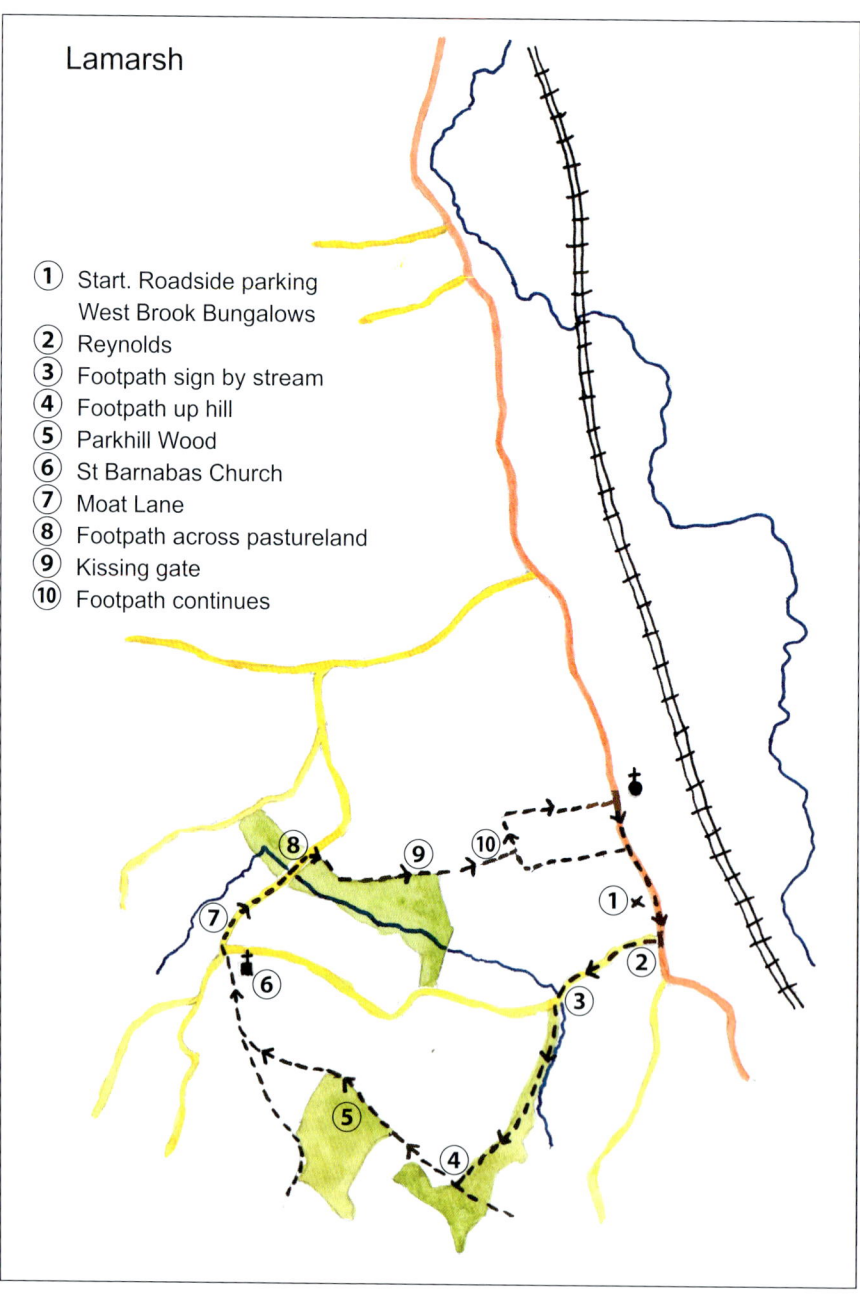

Manor House, Lamarsh

If you visit this little country church, with its avenue of pollarded lime trees and ancient porch, you will find carefully worked kneelers depicting flora and fauna as well as shuttered windows in the chancel.

In Alphamstone are more lovely old cottages, including Manor House with a lived-in feeling of chickens, footballs and cement mixer in the garden and a ladder leaning against the wall.

7. Look for Moat Lane, a narrow road that drops down where Prospect Cottages peep over a high hedge above steep banks of nettles, primroses and cow parsley.

When I walked here a blackbird sang from a horse chestnut tree whose sticky buds were just peeling themselves open. Pale yellow primroses peeped shyly from the verges.

You will pass Spring House on your left, with sloping lawns and a pond with yellow marsh marigolds, then Croft House. Next is an old barn beneath heavy pantiles with glimpses of its dark, shadowy interior. Then there's the stream again and more woodland.

Stour Valley

8. Just beyond the stream look for another footpath sign, half hidden in the hedge on the right. A sign says, 'Sheep. Please Close Gate.' Walk through more open pastureland where in spring blackthorn blossom smudges the hedges white.

9. Soon by a thick hedge you will see a kissing gate, pass through it (be ready for mud on wet days) and the view opens up again – where a buzzard circles, wings wide above the little houses in the valley. You are looking across the gentle landscape of the Stour Valley into Suffolk. Watch out and listen for the train, like a miniature railway.

10. The path dips and rises and leads you straight on keeping the hedge to your left. At a choice of paths turn left by some woodland a newly-dug sand could be a badger's sett. A few steps along here and you turn right walking down the side of the field which is to your left. You will be rewarded by the pastoral scene of the creamy coloured, round-towered church of the Holy Innocents with the backdrop of Suffolk fields and isolated farmsteads, tall masts and pylons that stride across the horizon.

Follow the field edge down to the valley. The Old Rectory (1909) with its gravel drive and neat lawns is on your right. Soon you will come to the road again where you turn right to head back to your starting place.

The Norman church, is nine hundred years old (in places). Inside is the cold, damp smell of old musty hymn books. There is an information board about round church towers.

You will pass the village hall, which was once a school and still has the bell and high windows to prove it. On the right by a row of bungalows is hopefully your car! Full of memories of this lovely part of North Essex head for Henny Swan – for a much needed comfort break.

During the day there is snack menu offering a good selection of sandwiches (including salmon and avocado) or soup with crusty bread served in the bar or garden as well a good choice of beers and yummy desserts such as Marmalade Bread Pudding with brandy custard. Short boat trips available at certain times if you fancy a trip on the river to end the day.

Lamarsh cottage

Walk 3: Great Sampford

A circular walk along narrow country roads, through fields and by a river, that both begins and finishes in the centre of the village.

Distance	2.6 miles or 4.3 km
Time	1½ hours at a gentle pace
Start	Park near to the Baptist Chapel in the main street
Terrain	Up and down, some steep climbs but not too demanding
Map	OS Explorer 195 Braintree & Saffron Walden
Refreshments	The Red Lion is closed for renovation at the moment but plans to re-open in Spring 2021. 01799 586010
Toilets	Public toilets by the village hall
Getting there	By car take the B1053 from Finchingfield to Saffron Walden which passes right through the village. No railway. No buses

1. Park beside the Baptist Church, opposite a long low thatched cottage appropriately called Churchside. Nearby is the Church of St Michael the Archangel within its brick wall. The lime trees were planted by General Eustace of Little Sampford Hall; the gentleman who liked to ride his horse up the stairs when he went to bed!

    Opposite is the Manor House built in 1595.

    Walk to the junction and take the road towards Finchingfield, a very pretty village just three miles away.

2. You will see Bull House – with a giveaway weather-vane. It was once The Black Bull Public house. You pass several pretty cottages and more modern houses. The Red Lion with painted signs on the grey bricks was closed

Great Sampford church and cottages   *Great Sampford houses*

when I walked this way but there are hopes that it will re-open again soon. It was built in 1830. There are picnic benches outside.

3. Next comes the Gt Sampford Board School – 1876, a red brick building of arched windows and doorways with interesting ridge tiles. Today it is still a village primary school. The School house is close by, with a tree laden with rosy apples (*Summer is coming to an end*). Monks Cottage is hidden behind a gate which opens onto a brick path. The house peeps out shyly from trees and shrubs in its garden.

4. Don't walk up Sparepenny Lane but at the bend cross the road and take Parsonage Farm Lane which climbs up and away from the village. This road is steep and little used judging by the moss that grows centrally. Walk past Monks Corner where bungalows cluster and see Snowdrop Cottage on your right.

A sign says Slow Down – not difficult. There are hedges either side but soon, when they cease, you can see across the fields of standing wheat. Views are becoming far reaching. A mixture of flowers grow along the verge, including gently scented Meadow Sweet- worthy of a pause to breath in its perfume.

5. You come to Birdbrook Cottage and Birdbrook House watching over the valley below. *A noisy aeroplane flew surprisingly low overhead – reminding me that we're not far from Stansted.* The road continues to climb with farmland either side. *The sun was warm.*

6. When you reach a footpath sign turn right into the extensive wheat field where a path has been cut that takes you to Hawkes Cottage. You walk level before it drops down to the hedge-line and ditch.

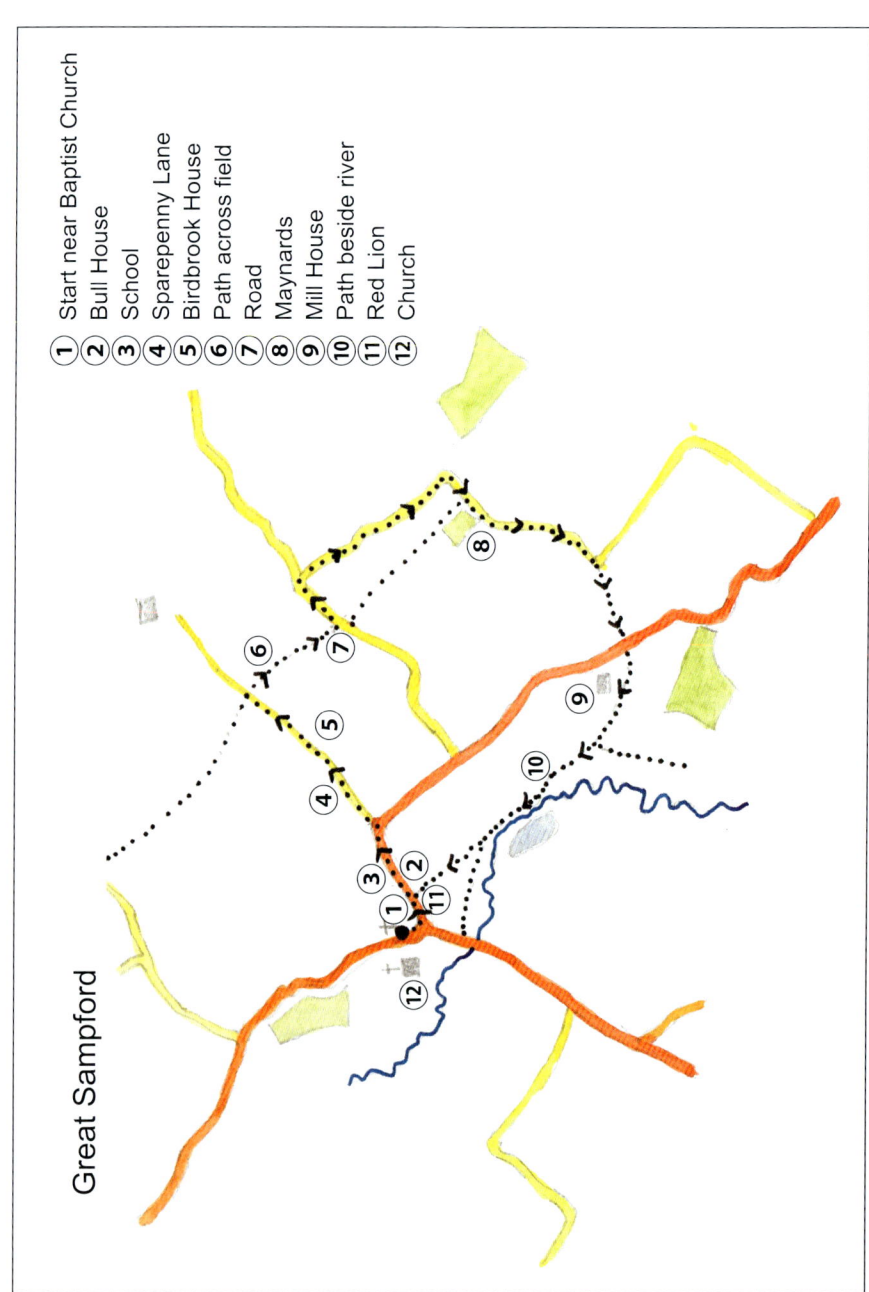

As I walked the sound of wheat cracking indicated that harvest was imminent.

A yellow arrow points the way under oak trees into another field where you continue straight forward. Pylons march into the far distance. Walk towards a thatched cottage and you come to a narrow road.

7. Turn left onto the tarmac road and follow it round until you reach the junction.

   (If you would like a shorter route you can cross over and follow a hedge-line which brings you out onto this same road, but my walk has a treat in store – especially in spring and summer.)

   When you see the white lines here, turn right and look out for a sign that tells you that these verges are managed as a roadside nature reserve for wildlife. Hence the tangle of wild flowers that bring rich colour to both sides of the quiet lane. Purple vetch and spears of yellow agrimony; brash dandelions and knapweed, cow mumble and fluffy thistle down spilling from fading flowers.

Sampford fields

The pylons continue to march ahead. Then comes the mewing call of buzzards and there they are, a pair, circling above the shadowy green Sampford Hall Wood to the left.

8. The lane curves and passes a big horse chestnut tree laden with conkers at Maynards, where there is a moat as well as weather-boarded barns. The Tudor house is half hidden from passers-by.

It seems that moats were dug in this area, not for defence but to keep fish, a welcome change at dinner time.

The road bends left and here you leave the road and turn right to walk by the field edge and then straight across the field itself.

It was clearly marked, but overgrown with weeds that made walking more difficult. But among them were scarlet pimpernels and delicate wild carrot. Here a painted lady butterfly graciously alighted on the path and closed her lovely wings to become invisible. I paused in wonder. Ahead the fields dipped into the valley and rose to clumps of woodland and yet more fields. A lovely sight with towering white clouds in a pale blue sky.

9. You come to a hedge line and the end of the field and another footpath sign. Here is a main road where you can see a green painted cottage beneath a slate roof on the right.

Mill House

I walk up the daisy-lined path and knock at the door of Mill House, where a Lion and a Unicorn adorn the walls. This is the home of a botanical artist whom I was hoping to meet, but alas, no-one is at home.

Cross the road and find the footpath by the boundary hedge of the garden. Here is another field and a footpath marching across it. To the right you can see The Grange and the Old Rectory across the fields. The path drops down into the valley of the river Pant.

10. You come to nettles and brambles, so take care as you enter a grassy stretch that borders the meandering river. The meadow has football goals. Ignore the stile and the footbridge and keep going straight forward towards the village.

Another buzzard suddenly lifted himself from a tree and flapped over our heads. We could see the barred pattern on his wings.

You come to a stile and the path curves with the river at the lower end of the meadow. You pass an ancient willow tree.

Some carefully planted trees in very straight lines form a copse on your right. A bank marks the site of a reservoir on the left – which is dry now, we are told.

In front of you the houses of the village appear. Follow the path over a plank bridge at a ditch where another sign points the way. Here a yellow arrow directs you right towards the houses, with the hedge on your right. Then divert diagonally across the field until you come to back gardens where geraniums flower in pots on patios and conservatories offer comfort and warmth. Washing flutters on whirligig lines and another footbridge appears to take you between high fences.

11. At the road you turn left and ahead you can see the Red Lion pub with 'Ridleys Fine Ales' painted upon its walls. Walk towards it and you will find yourself on familiar ground for this is where we began.

Red Lion Inn

12. If you have time to visit the church turn right towards churchyard near the Obelisk to Colonel Jonas Watson who died in 1741. Inside the church you can learn more about this gentleman – who so faithfully served king and country with great honour.

There are other lichen blotched gravestones including one to William Ruffle, 1881. He was a local legend in the village as the shop-keeper, police constable and clerk for over fifty years.

A notice in the church porch tells you that it is open from 10am - 3.pm every day and yes, the heavy door is not locked. Inside it is cool and echoing. There are towering arches spanning the chancel and nave and huge pillars. It seems very spacious with sunlight and shadows playing through latticed clear glass windows. I discover there was an earlier church on this site – the presence of Stow Farm nearby is a give-way for Stow means holy place, indeed, this big church was built between 1320-1350 – a designated deanery church, serving some twenty parishes.

There is a crudely carved school master's desk and a note that once the village school met here in the church – stopping in 1770. The desk we see is believed to be the original one used. There are old iron hinges to a small cupboard with a note inside; 'Curiosity killed the cat!'

If you are in need of refreshment and loos – the picture postcard village of Finchingfield is but three miles away. Here are cafés galore.

Walk 4: Foxearth

There has been a settlement here since Domesday – a village built around local agriculture, seven miles from Halstead and seven miles from Sudbury. Clearly it was known in Saxon times as the place where the foxes lived.

Distance	2.75 miles or 4.5 km
Time	Approximately 1 hour
Start	In the centre of the village somewhere near the Foxearth sign
Terrain	Only gentle slopes, mainly flat
Map	OS Explorer 196 Sudbury, Hadleigh & Dedham Vale
Refreshments	Facilities to make a cuppa in the church. Nearby Long Melford has plenty of tea rooms and pubs serving food
Toilets	None
Getting there	Take the B1064 from Sudbury to Long Melford and turn left at the crossroads towards Borley and Foxearth. Cross the river Stour and bear right then left to reach Foxearth. No buses

I visited Foxearth in late September and parked my car outside Hall Cottage. Beyond the ivy curling along the brick wall stood an apple tree laden with fruit. The village sign was nearby bearing the inevitable fox, of course.

Foxearth village sign

1. Find the Foxearth sign and take the road to Long Melford. You soon will pass the Old School with a gabled porch and ornate

Foxearth cottages

windows in the flint walls. Look out for the Old School House and the pretty thatched cottages that line the road. You will come to tall gates and a driveway leading to Foxearth House. Here is the Lodge.

2. Take the footpath on your left by the notice board of the church – St Peter and Paul. You find yourself walking through an avenue of lime trees until you reach a double hedge and the sturdy lych-gate where there is a footbridge over a dry ditch into the churchyard. There is space here to rest the coffin before the burial. (Lych comes from *lycche* – medieval word for body).

I wandered into the overgrown churchyard with clipped ancient yew trees and tall limes and the tinny echo of the clock on the tower chiming the hour. This was a land of shadows. Jackdaws circled and landed on the roof. I found the porch and the door was not locked. Soon I had the kettle steaming and made myself a cup of coffee – kindly left for visitors.

3. Stop to explore the church in part eight hundred years old but mainly rebuilt in Victoria times. Its walls are of knapped black flints, often gathered from the fields by local women and children. The north aisle is dated 1350 and the chancel 1450, but the west tower is 1862.

There was once a spire some one hundred and thirty feet high, a landmark for miles around but lightning brought it crashing to the ground in a freak summer storm.

Inside I found a stained glass window commemorating three sisters, Isabel and Anne Foster and Mary aged sixteen, twenty and nineteen. It was their father, the rector who paid for the restoration in 1863. Look for the ornate reredos, gilded organ, glazed tiles and the wall paintings of saints and martyrs, beneath the heavily decorated ceiling for this is a place of patterns; they accost you whichever way you turn. The choir stalls too are decorated, delicately carved with pious angels.

There was damson jam and courgette chutney for sale – proceeds to the organ fund. There are plaques to pilots and navigators and outside a First World War Memorial which includes the name of Nurse Ileene Carter who is buried nearby to the right of the porch. But her name is omitted from the plaque in the porch. I wonder why? She was a local girl whose father was a brewer at Ward and Sons. She lived in the thatched cottage opposite the bus shelter. I also see the name of George Balaam – appropriately named – a shepherd at Foxearth Hall.

4. Follow a yellow arrow sign passing more recent graves until you come to a gap in the hedge behind the church. Then keeping the hedge to your right, with a field to your left, leave the churchyard behind and walk across the field. The red bricked house of Cardinal's Farm is to your right. The path rises and soon you are in a wide open space. You reach a narrow road that climbs gently to the sky line.

Cardinal's Farm

A buzzard soared in the sky above the buildings of Foxearth Hall to my left. I paused to look back at the rooftops of the village beyond the rolling farmland. Scabious and yarrow flowered by the hedge where old man's beard tangled itself among the red berries. Soon I can see a faraway view of Long Melford with a little church on the horizon to my right. Directly

Foxearth

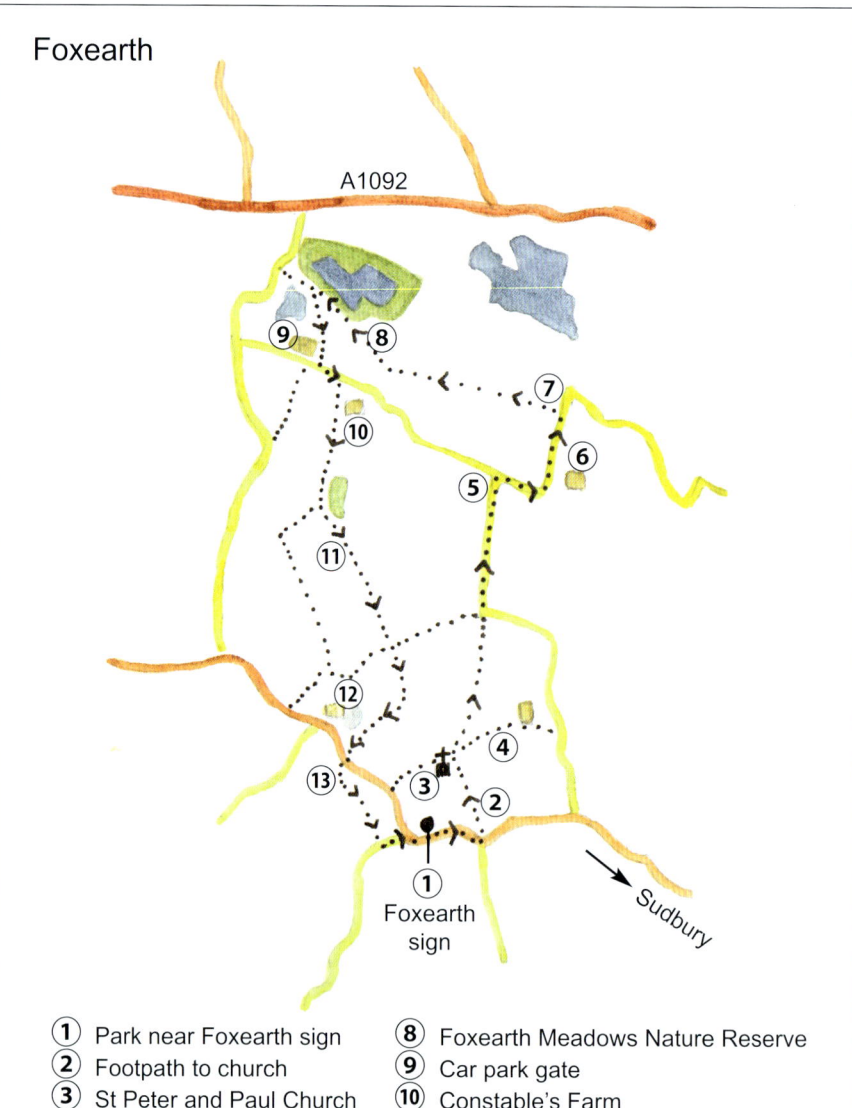

1. Park near Foxearth sign
2. Footpath to church
3. St Peter and Paul Church
4. Cardinals' Farm
5. T-junction to Long Melford
6. Weston Hall
7. Steep steps up bank
8. Foxearth Meadows Nature Reserve
9. Car park gate
10. Constable's Farm
11. Footpath beyond copse
12. Foxearth Hall and Moat
13. Footpath behind houses back to road

ahead I can see Glemsford in the distance. A low thatched cottage peeps over a hedge-line. Indeed this is a scenic spot!

5. At the T-junction a signpost points you to Long Melford. The narrow road drops down into the valley. You pass a seat dedicated to 'Clive who loved this place'. Here is Weston Cottage and Weston Hall Farm.

6. Then comes Weston Hall itself with tall octagonal chimneys and a moat. The road drops between high banks.

7. When you see steep steps and a metal handrail on your left – this is the footpath to take – but there are no marker posts and be warned – it is a huge field to cross.

    I tramped across the field – stumbling over the uneven corrugated surface – not sure of the exact route of the footpath – clearly marked on the map. It seemed to go on forever but when I eventually reached the far hedge I found a gap with a sign bearing a yellow arrow. Relief!

Weston Hall

Huge field Foxearth

8. Now you find yourself in Foxearth Meadows Nature Reserve, an eleven acre site of wetland meadows and ponds, once gravel pits. An information board reads that here you may see otters, comma butterflies and kingfishers or even hear a nightingale in late April or May. This is an important site for dragonflies and damselflies – up to twenty-two species have been seen here; vibrant electric-blue emperors and brown hawkers

among them. Follow the path to the far metal gate, keeping the hazel hedges to your left.

The path is overgrown and wet with heavy dew. Stalks of seeding cow mumble offer a scaffold where spiders drape their silvery webs. Fleabane flowers glow yellow in the grass amidst wild mint and rustling rushes edge the ponds. There is a bench where I sit, hopefully awaiting a kingfisher – but no kingfisher comes!

9. The gate marks the boundary of the Reserve a yellow arrow sign on a post points past bicycle stands and a small car park – only open in summer months. Beyond it is a little road.

10. Turn left and begin to climb the hill until you see steep steps on the right that take you to – yes, another ploughed field! Look for Constable Farm to your left.

This too you must cross, though when I walked here there were boot-marks to show me the route. Not only is it hard going – but it's uphill! Soon my

Constable's Farm

legs are aching! A jay screeches in the trees that surround Constable's Farm on the left. The view makes the plod worthwhile.

11. At the hedge is another yellow arrow on a post. In the dry ditch nettles and brambles grow. Turn left to walk along the field edge following a grassy path. You pass a small copse. Keep the hedge to your left – together with a line of telegraph poles.

12. Foxearth Hall is on the right. The path drops to a stile then travels between a fence and a hedge to another high stile and the corner of a field. Cross one of many wooden footbridges over a stream. Negotiate a kissing-gate and take care at the unfenced moat.

Shaggy highland cattle raise their heads with huge bicycle-handle horns to stare at me as I near them. Geese too graze on the cropped grass.

13. Look for *another* yellow arrow, *another* wooden footbridge and *another* gate. The path leads beside houses to the road. Go straight over to a footpath sign pointing along a field edge with more gardens to your left. There is another footbridge and soon you turn left to walk between a high laurel hedge and a fence. This leads back to the road, your starting place and the centre of the village where you parked the car. Turn left and pass a house called Mole Hall with a central chimney stack and curious tiles on the roof.

Mole Hall, Foxearth

This was once the home of Evans the blacksmith. Sadly three of his sons are also named on the War Memorial. I stop to reflect upon the sorrow that these walls must have held during those dreadful days. And so my walk ends on an unusually sombre note.

Walk 5: Navestock

This rural parish is only fifty kilometres. from central London yet has the sense of somewhere remote and forgotten. The road access is complicated and there is no bus route, perhaps this is why?

Distance	2.7 miles or 4.5 km. A circular walk mainly along shadowy lanes with a stopping place on route
Time	1½ hours
Start	Park by Navestock Heath
Terrain	Some long steep inclines
Map	OS Explorer 175 Southend & Basildon
Refreshments	Norpar – a converted farmyard has barns where snacks are usually served all year round; 01277 374968; Norpar.co.uk
Toilets	None on route but Norpar has toilets
Getting there	Take the A1023 at junction 28 of the M25 to find a left turning into the road for Navestock. Drive along country roads for about 5 miles to reach Navestock Heath. No buses or train

1. Park near Heath Cottage at the edge of the heath, a stretch of open space full of wild flowers and creatures. Walk along the top of the heath, look for Randalls Cottages to confirm your way.

   In *the sea of wild seeding grasses white butterflies danced. Vetches curled their tentacles around sedges and cow parsley and golden buttercups contrasted with vivid blue cornflowers.*

2. At the crossroads turn right into Murthering Lane. The left turning – Old Road takes you along the other side of the heath – perhaps explore it later?

You soon see a pond full of tall rushes opposite the Old General Stores, or Forge or Post Office – a house confused about its identity, perhaps?

3. Turn right towards Shonks Mill into Mill Lane (or is it Bounce Hill) and like me enjoy the quirky names we are encountering.

The narrow lane crept between high hedges on either side where dog roses flowered amidst hazel, hornbeam and field maple. Long white letters ordered SLOW. (I'm not sure how anyone would go fast here!) The shadowy lane dropped and here and there when gaps appeared lovely views of patchwork fields, where pylons marched into the distance,

Navestock signpost

became visible over young green wheat, though the day we walked was grey and hazy. The lane became a green tree tunnel as it curved then climbed. Giant leaves of burdock and tall nettles added to the overgrown feeling as oak trees towered above us.

4. The road curves and dips steeply. A sign at Rye Etch warns us that guard dogs run beyond the barbed wire fence on the right.

To confirm it, an unseen dog yapped as we passed where the road rose and fell with the land. In a garden on the right were raspberries and blackcurrants and soon clumps of foxgloves appeared.

5. A purple house stands on the right and ahead is Miller's Cottage where red roses grow around the porch in summer. Although there is a footpath sign pointing left, here we turn right to reach a T-junction, Shonks Mill Lane and bridge. The mill ceased working in 1860 and has since been demolished. Pause to enjoy the river where a weeping willow trails its branches into the flowing river Roding.

In 1566 Shonks Mill Bridge was in danger of collapse. Its timbers were rotten. A wrangle ensued – who was responsible? At last it agreed and rebuilt in 1641.

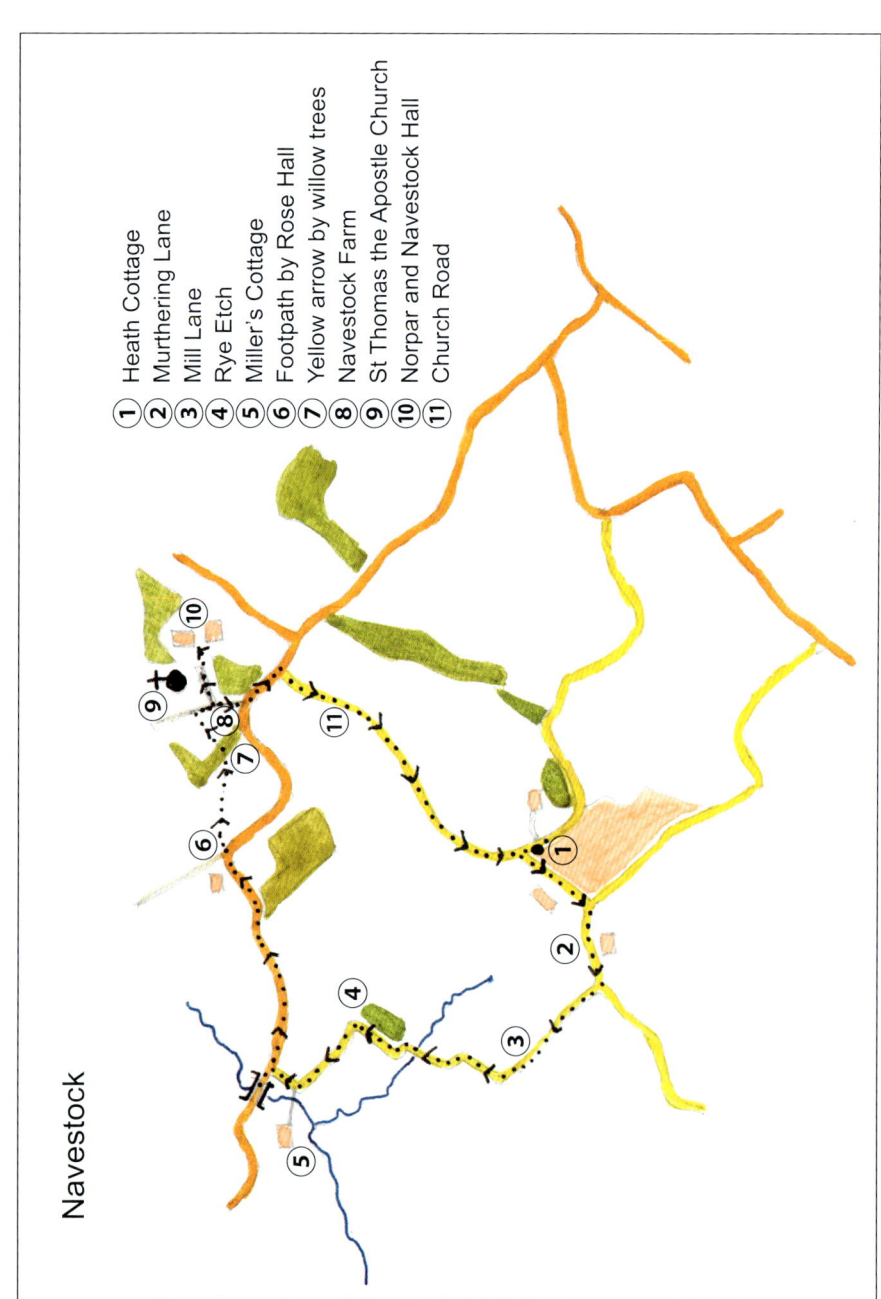

Miller's Cottage Navestock

6. Turn right towards Roding and walk up the hill of this road which can be busy at times. Take care, there is little verge and only white lines edge the road. You cross another bridge and see a house on your left with honey coloured chimney pots on a slate roof; One and Two Rose Hall. It sits on a bend which is where we find our footpath, just beyond it on the left.

7. Walk by the house to find the path that goes through the hedge and crosses a wheat field. This stretch could be muddy after rain, though pebbles and flints dot the bare earth. Ahead you will see willow trees. (A jay screeched as we walked here.) Look out for a yellow arrow where the footpath goes left through overgrown nettles and goose grass. Try to avoid being stung.

8. Now Navestock Hall Farm is seen on your right. In the grounds are tennis courts and a trampoline but a thick laurel hedge does its best to obscure the gardens from curious people like me. On the left is a small stream and at a private sign look for a wooden footbridge to cross it. Again the path was overgrown with long grass and a riot of thistles and pink campion (plum puddings – country name) but fight your way to the stile, keeping your eye on the church spire ahead. You enter paddocks where horses graze.

The horses pricked their ears forward with interest when we appeared and ambled to greet us, tails swishing away the countless flies that pestered them.

Navestock church

9. Keeping a hedge on your left walk up to another stile and footbridge and here you will find the little church of St Thomas the Apostle with its notable wooden tower and shingled spire. There is a bench if you need a rest.

The day we walked here coincided with a traveller's funeral. A horse drawn carriage clopped along the road with many people walking behind it in silence. A pall bearer told us that the church was packed to the doors so we were unable to peep inside. He said, "they'll be there for hours".

The little church of flint rubble and pebbles seems to squat amidst the surrounded woodland. The north wall of the nave is dated as early as the 11th century. On 21st September 1940 a German land mine damaged the church but it was completely restored in 1954. The bomb crater has become the garden of Remembrance.

10. Facing the church turn right to walk down the track to a pebbledash cottage where a sign directs you to Norpar Barns and Navestock Hall a few steps further on. This is a good place to stop for a drink, cake and loo. The barns are to the left of the Elizabethan timber-framed hall, presumably,

judging by the stable block, once the farm yard. Here, surrounded by scented roses in summer you can enjoy a rest. There is a greenhouse to buy succulents, a barn of candles and pretty pottery jugs, brimming with dried flowers and berries.

After my scone, thick with cream and jam and hot chocolate served in the 14th century barn, I took

Navestock Hall

the brick steps to peer inside the granary museum, a barn on mushroom stilts. As the shop assistant kindly unlocked the door for me she told me that the hall had been bombed in the Second World War and much had been rebuilt. She continued, "Norpar is a combination of Norwood and Parish, the names of the owner. Originally we sold only dried and silk flowers now there are accessories for home and garden. From mid-October we start Christmas with a seasonal barn where you can make wreaths."

The inside of the museum was full of shadows but packed with cobwebbed farm implements; old sieves, milk churns, a wooden yoke and a rusty scythe. It smelt of hay and dust. There were paraffin lamps on a beam and a mangle stood by the entrance.

As I left I saw a blue WC sign on a latched door in another barn. Within was an old fashioned, but clean toilet.

11. Walk down the lane to reach a busier road where you turn left. On your right a stream runs in a ditch. Take the right turning to Navestock Heath. This is Church Road and is the beginning of a long, steady climb between trees and thick hedges. The views on either side are lovely, when you can see them! You are on the home stretch.

You pass some semi-detached cottages on your left then 'Marleys', a house out of sight, before you see the Heath stretching out before you and hopefully your car!

Walk 6: Great and Little Henny

These villages are just two miles south of Sudbury and the River Stour – the county boundary. In the 1830s the population of Great Henny peaked at about 400 souls – mainly agricultural folk. In those days there were two day schools. But for the last two hundred years less than two hundred people have lived here.

Distance	4.6 km or 2.8 miles. A circular up-and-down walk in the far north of Essex starting at Great Henny and calling on Little Henny to enjoy both beautiful scenery and woodland
Time	1½ hours
Start	Great Henny Parish Reading Room
Terrain	Some gentle slopes in the undulating land
Map	OS Explorer 196 Sudbury, Hadleigh & Dedham Vale
Refreshments	Henny Swan 01787 367953 hennyswan@gmail.com It is advisable to book but not essential. Wickham St Paul: Spencer's Farm and Coffee Shop 01787 267977 spencersfarmshop.com and The Victory Inn at the Ship 01787 269 364 thevictoryinn.com (both closed Mondays)
Toilets	In these venues above, none on route
Getting there	Take the A131 between Halstead and Sudbury. The Hennys are signposted from this road. Head for Clay Hill and the Church. No buses

1. Park your car by the Parish Reading Room near a bench dedicated to Hugh Kennedy McIntyre who gave 85 years of his time and love to this community. Look for a sign to the church and follow the narrow road past Fuchsia Cottage where a fox stares gloomily from his door knocker. In early autumn pale pears hang from a tree in the garden.

Across the field the church spire points skyward while to your left the land falls to the valley and rises beyond it. Beautiful!

2. Look for Thorncroft Farm nestling in the valley.

3. Now you will come to the carved lych-gate of the church of St Mary the Virgin. Tramp up the gravel path and hopefully the door will be unlocked. If so you are in for a treat. The lower stages of the tower are late 11th century, but the building was rebuilt in the 14th century using flint rubble and restored in the 19th century. Look for ancient scratchings of crosses on the arched doorway and a 16th century parish chest in the tower, with arcaded panels. It is thought to be Italian. There are two 14th century windows in the nave and another in the bell chamber. Outside is a pump close to the porch.

Henny Parish Rooms

Henny view

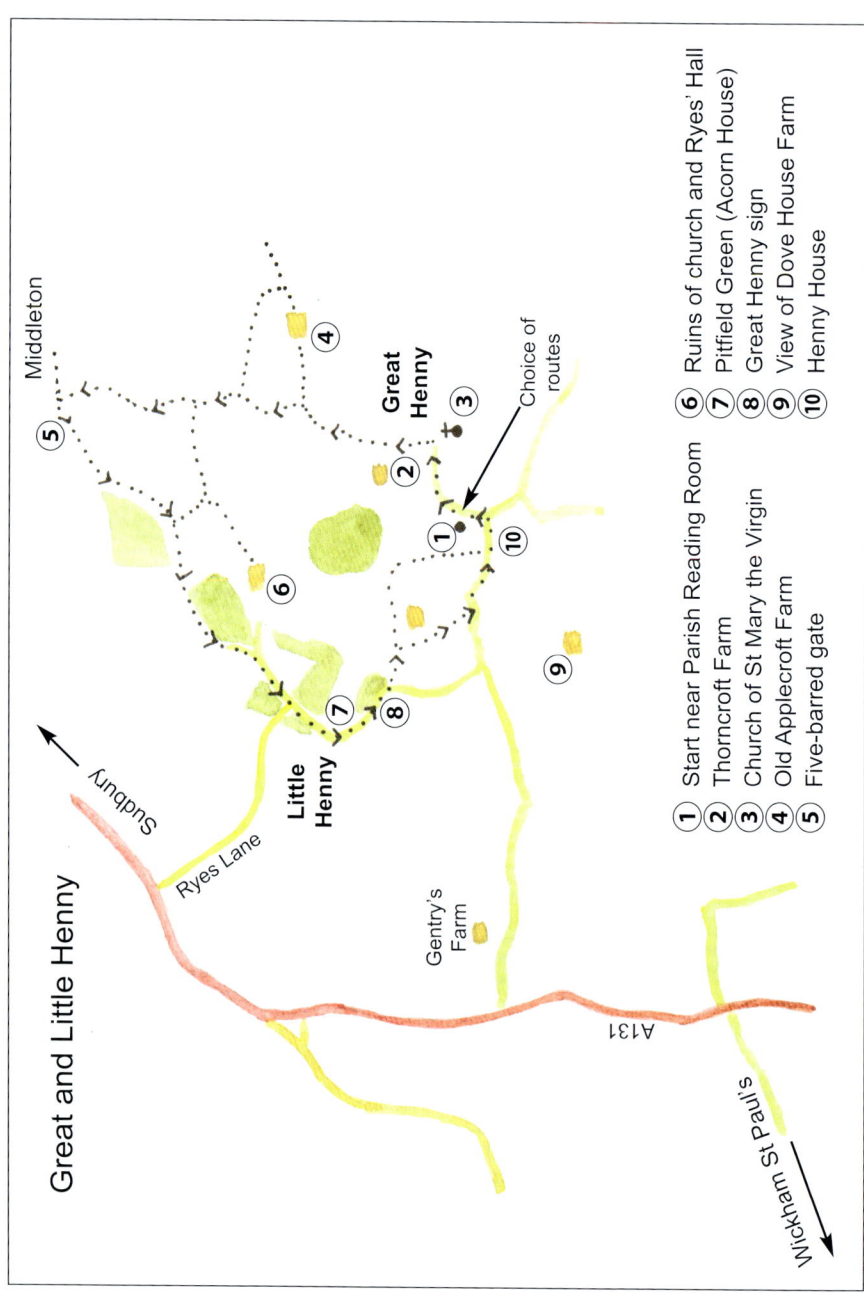

In the porch were jars of jam and greengage conserve for sale. I pushed open the heavy door and walked over the floor slab of Thomas Sewell 1702 (with his shield of arms), to the tiled floor of the altar. A brass eagle gleamed and I noticed amusing carvings of medieval musicians in the roof, adorning the beam ends. Two fearsome demons guarded the entrance to the chancel. I paused before the brass to William Fyscher and his wife, Anne and count the children; six sons and nine daughters. Goodness me!

There is a framed picture of vicars including the youngest Edward Harbottle-Grimstone, sixteen years of age! The record goes back to 1270 and the first rector here.

Henny churchgate

Wander back to the lych-gate and find the footpath sign of St Edmund's Way. It is near 'The Old Hatchery'. Here is a shadowy path dropping between the garden and a hedge to reach a field.

The field had been ploughed and brown soil stretched away to the right. I could smell the warm scent of horses.

You will come to some barns where cobwebs thick with dust drape themselves across the windows. Then you will see a house and stables. Look out for a walnut tree. According to the map this is Thorncroft Farm. Bear left to climb a high stile and walk by the side of a meadow with a hedge on your right. By a beech tree is another stile which takes you into rough pastureland.

Amongst the untidy seeding grasses, pale pink and white clovers added gentle colour.

4. You reach a foot bridge over a dry ditch, then cross another field. Look out for a great oak tree to your right and yellow arrows to confirm the route. The buildings to your right belong to Old Applecroft Farm.

There is another footpath here if you'd like to take a 2 mile diversion and extend your walk to stop at Henny Swan. It passes the 16th century (or even earlier) farmhouse with clay peg tile roof. In the 19th century the timber framed building was clad with flint-work and brick.

Now you begin to climb – quite steeply and lovely views appear as the land rises with sweeping curves. If you need a rest you will soon reach a bench dedicated to Amanda MacDonald – 'her little bit of heaven'.

Ahead to my right, I could see the faraway Stour Valley and Suffolk where pylons marched across the horizon. The path dropped down to a muddy puddle then into another field where it climbed again, with woodland to the right. I stopped to look back – the church spire poked up above the trees. Now I followed a line of oak trees up the sloping hillside. A swallow skimmed over the scooped out land to my left and there was a lovely sense of space with stunning views in all directions.

5. At a five-barred gate on the ridge of the hill, you **don't** drop down to Middleton directly ahead instead turn left and follow the hedge line into green shadows and woodland.

Great Henny countryside

The path drops steeply by a sandy bank – the domain of many rabbits – judging by the gaping dark holes amidst the tree roots. Or badgers perhaps?

You cross a stream where a twisted willow has fallen onto the metal poles of the footbridge. The path begins to climb again then narrows.

There are nettles and ferns in late summer and red haws ripening in the hedge and a gravelly crunch under my boots as I pass Scots pines creating stripy lines of shadow across my route. The first yellow leaves have fallen. A startled blackbird swoops into the dappled green world of woodland. If I painted the scene I would need a stipple brush to create flecks of yellow and streaks of light.

On the left is a gateway – Forestry Commission land. Then comes Home Wood to the left and a paddock to the right heralding Rye Croft Cottages of red brick with heavy pan-tiled roof. You soon reach the road.

6. To the left are the ruins of Little Henny Church down a private driveway to The Ryes.

   The foundations were excavated in 1929 to reveal late 12th century walls, one metre thick. The church was destroyed by fire in the late 16th century.

   You will see a red post-box – here you bear right onto a tarmacked road between high fences which brings you to a junction where you turn left. This is Little Henny. Look for Henny Lodge (left).

7. At Pitfield Green you will find Acorn House with a flag pole.

8. Then you see a farmyard and some abandoned cars half hidden by scrawling brambles. Here is the Great Henny sign standing amidst a heap of hardcore! Turn left to walk along a gravel drive where specimen trees grow in neat borders. Look out for the Old Rectory and for a pond with tall rushes.

   Bear right at a gateway and walk on a grassy stretch with a high hedge on your right and a fence on your left.

9. *A lovely view opened up across the valley as blue-grey smoke drifted from a garden bonfire. Dove House Farm was in sight where a little road climbed and curved. Again pylons, like steel giants straddled the horizon.*

Henny landscape

The path falls gently down to a By-Way sign pointing back the way you came. Then you reach Clay Hill Road. Turn left and take a leg-aching climb up the steep slope. Now you are heading back to the village.

On the left you will see The Old Rectory through a gap in the hedge. Then you come to Clay Hill Cottages where we are reminded to; 'Slow down – Children and Pets'.

10. Look for Henny House on your right and very soon the Parish Rooms will appear – and hopefully, your car! Before you finish the walk, explore a little further along the road to see the pretty 17th century 'Thatched Cottage' with a brick path, behind a picket fence.

For refreshments you have a choice; take a short drive back to the A131. Cross the road to go to Wickham St Paul for a choice of 'eateries' or head east for the Stour river valley and Henny Swan.

Walk 7: Terling

Not far from the busy A12 and the town of Witham is this little gem of a village, Terling (pronounced Tarling), where the soothing sound of the River Ter is heard as it meanders gently through the parish. A circular walk that begins and ends in the centre of the village which explores narrow roads and crosses pastureland.

Distance	2.7 miles or 4.4 km
Time	1½ hours
Start	By the village hall, close to the school on an unmade track
Terrain	Fairly gentle rise and fall
Map	OS Explorer 183 Chelmsford & The Rodings
Refreshments	Rayleigh Arms 01245 233444 info@therayleigharms.co.uk Serving lunch and evening meals and take-aways. Please check before you come
Toilets	The Rayleigh Arms
Getting there	Leave the A12 at Hatfield Peverel to take the Terling road, or from Witham take the Terling road to Powers Hall End

1. Look for the track to the village hall where you find the Victorian school. This is a good place to leave your car. Walk down towards the bridge and river. You will see the village hall on your right, among other things licensed for wrestling! The footpath arrow points straight on, though the road is private.

2. Cross the river Ter by an old brick bridge. The route begins to

Cottages overlooking Gamble's Green

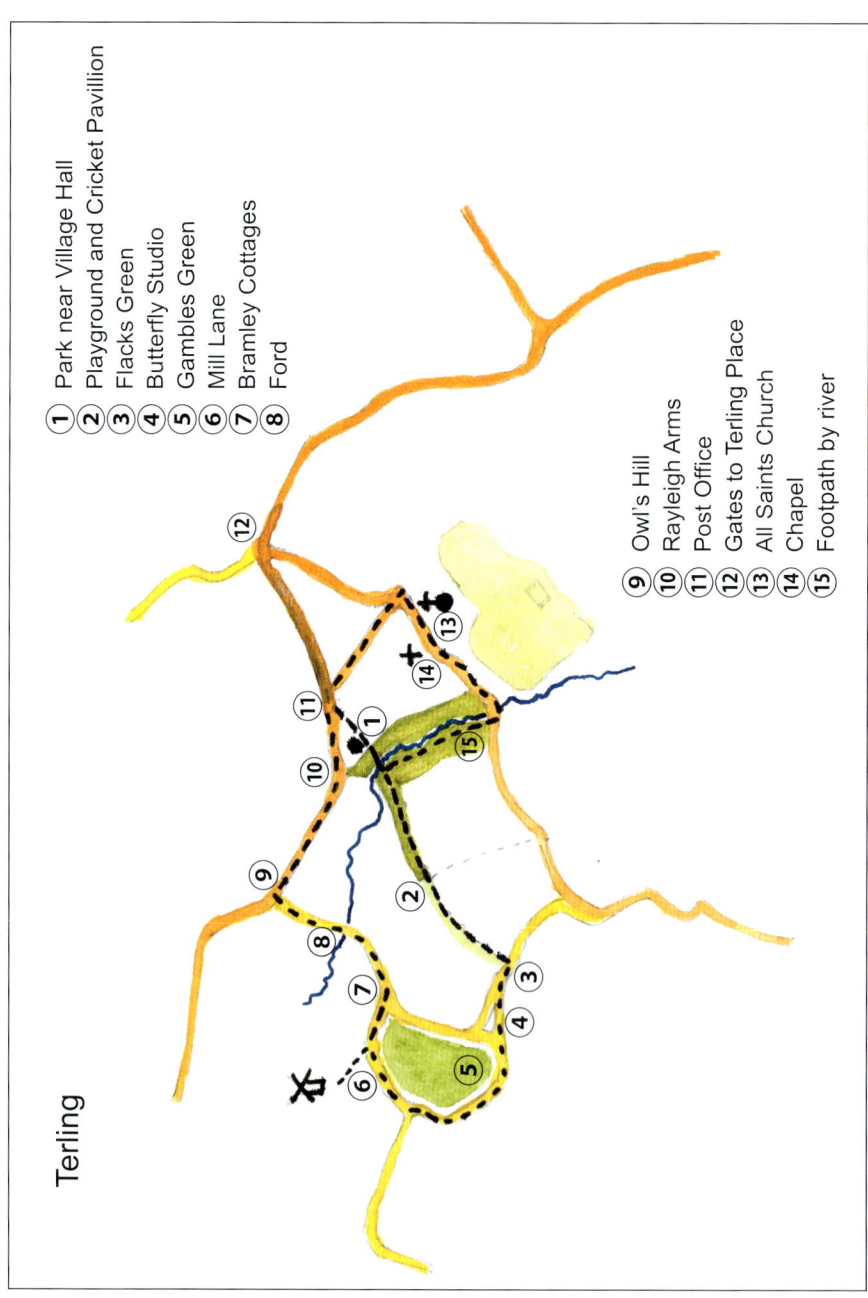

climb gently. Pass the Tennis Club and children's playground to your left, while trees edge the path on your right. Keep straight on passing the Cricket Pavilion until you reach the road and Flack's Green.

3. At the gate turn right then bear left where the road forks around the central grassy area dotted with brown molehills! There is a house called The Hedges.

4. The Butterfly Studio offers art and craft workshops. It stands behind The Coffee House with yellow jasmine flowering about the gate. I am curious about this name, but no-one is at home.

5. Follow the road past Meadow Cottage, with its thatch and brick driveway, then the road curves and you find yourself in Gambles Green overlooked by several pretty cottages. One is called Marchants. It has charming latticed windows and a well in the front garden. The road curves right again. The White House has some interesting pargetting designs including a willow tree, a shield and a plough. Take Hull Lane on the right. Now comes a line of semi-detached houses sporting satellite dishes. Most gardens have elaborate bird-feeders too.

The Coffee House

6. Here you need a short diversion along Mill Lane if you want to see the windmill. Walk by Jacaranda Cottage with a deep peg-tiled roof and three tiny dormers before you come to the white weather-boarded windmill itself. Today it is no longer working but has become a private house. The gates are open and you get a good view as it tapers away to a silver cap.

7. Retrace your steps to Hull Lane and turn left to continue the walk by red-bricked Bramley Cottages. Look out for a monkey puzzle tree in one garden. At the end of this lane is a small triangle of grass with a central post-box, here you turn left into Norman Hill. You will pass the Old Rectory of grey brick, then Kendalls, a peachy-coloured house with a gable at one end. Ahead are more brick cottages with slate roofs.

Terling Mill

In February I saw the welcome first signs of spring, snowdrops and purple crocuses in several gardens and the sun felt warm again.

8. Now the road falls down to the ford where signs warn motorists not to attempt to drive their cars through it. Local stories tell that several adventurous souls have regretted taking this route! There is an iron footbridge, with a chipped painted railing and it is worth pausing here to enjoy the gentle sound of the water as it trickles over pebbles and small rocks. Someone has thoughtfully placed a bench here if you care to take a rest. The water is surprisingly deep and clear.

As I stood here, enjoying the birdsong I heard the drumming sound of a woodpecker somewhere in the trees. Later in the Rayleigh Arms I saw a delightful photograph of long-ago children playing in the ford.

9. The road slopes upwards and soon you turn right into Owl's Hill. Now there are houses on both sides of the road; Viner Cottages, set well back on your left. You come to a telephone box – now serving as a defibrillator.

10. You will pass Raisling's House with a line of neat flower tubs outside and the black and white Owl's Hill House with its impressive central chimney, standing behind black iron railings. The road drops down to The Rayleigh Arms ahead on your left – a substantial grey brick building. This is a good place to stop for some refreshment.

Inside are both comfy sofas and solid wooden dining tables. The menu offered a special price for pensioners which was very reasonable. The staff wore T-shirts bearing a logo The Monkey and there is a photograph of a monkey by the bar. My curiosity was aroused. As I waited for a bowl of carrot and coriander soup, I asked a friendly waitress to tell me about the pub.

The Rayleigh Arms

The view from my seat in the bay window looks back on the cottages of the village. And the monkey? Well this was the name given to the Rayleigh Arms by the locals, because of a story about a monkey saving lives at Terling Place – the home of the Strutt family.

11. From the Rayleigh Arms take the road uphill to The Street. Again it passes several interesting cottages, one of which served as the Post Office. At the end of this road you reach a junction. Here the present Post Office and Village Stores is on your left. It is an old Tudor house. The side which now houses the Post Office used to be a slaughter house and butcher's shop.

12. Bear right at the junction and by Butler's Lodge you will see the cone-topped gates of Terling Place. The gravel drive (marked private) leads to the Grade II listed Georgian mansion but as there are belts of trees surrounding this estate you can only see it from a distance across the fields. The current house replaced the former Terling Place (1597) but we know people have lived here from time immemorial for in 1824 a gardener

dug up Roman silver and golden coins. This has been the home of the Strutt family for generations. John Strutt had the 200 acre parkland landscaped with three avenues of trees and a ha-ha enclosing the pleasure garden. In 1821 Colonel Joseph Strutt became the first Lord Rayleigh.

I read that the grounds are open to the public two or three times a year. I must find out when. On the way home I stopped to get a photograph of Terling Place across pastureland from a gateway by the road side.

13. A few steps further takes you to All Saints church which reveals the longstanding presence of the Strutt family in Terling. Edward Gerald Strutt was an agriculturalist, 'wise and trusted; a man of great heart' and John William Strutt was a 'constant worshipper in the church'. Part of the church is 15th century but the tower was rebuilt in 1732 – funded partly by the Strutt family. There is a fine wooden porch, built in Tudor times and some lovely old brasses inside. However a 13th century lancet window only visible outside betrays an earlier church on the site. A boundary wall in the churchyard marks the beginning of the Terling Hall Estate.

Terling Place

Tudor house close to the church.

Nearby stands a wonderful 15th century timber framed house behind a mossy red-bricked wall. There is a neatly clipped box hedge in the garden.

The setting is almost perfect, with another broad green space stretching out before me. Jackdaws circling around the tower and settling on the church roof fill the air with their noisy call.

14. Over the green stands Terling Congregational Chapel built of decorative red brick in 1688. The final stages of our walk takes you past it and down the road towards the river again. Look out for The Wooden Cottage – like something from a story book. The road falls away.

15. You will come to a permitted footpath that turns right and follows the course of the shallow river. In early spring you will be rewarded with snow drops under the willow trees. This is a pleasant ending for any walk – especially when the trees are full of birdsong. The path leads back to the bridge where the walk began. Turn right to return to your starting place.

Walk 8: Matching Tye

Long ago the Saxon tribe of Maecca settled in West Essex. Today their homestead is known as Matching. This easy, circular walk takes you from Matching Tye through Newman's End, to Matching itself. The nearby pretty village of Matching Green, a short drive away, is also well worth a stop before you go home. This is pure Essex farmland, mainly arable today but in 1610 dairy herds grazed here and people paid their tithes in cheeses. Brick making was also important and there were several kilns.

Distance	2.8 miles or 4.6 km
Time	1½ hours
Start	Rainbow Road or any roadside spot nearby
Terrain	Fairly even – but a few gentle slopes
Map	OS Explorer 183 Chelmsford & The Rodings
Refreshments	The Fox Inn in Matching Tye is open and serves food. 01279 731335 www.the foxinn.com
Toilets	Sorry. No public toilets
Getting there	The M11 is very near. Take the A1060 to Hatfield Heath and then the Matching Road to – well, Matching of course. The SB12 bus from Harlow passes once a day – but not at weekends

1. In Matching Tye there is no public car park so you need to find a safe roadside spot to park the car. Opposite the turning to Carter's Green you will see Rainbow Road. This is where my walk starts.

   Go along Rainbow Road to the corner where you will see the footpath sign which points you beside a fence and into a wide open field with far-reaching views, including the fast flowing stream of cars on the M11.

I walked straight across the stubble - prickly bristle on the face of the field - and a huge field too. Tiny blue dots of speedwell and scarlet pimpernels decorated the pathway beneath my boots and the sound of traffic floated across from the busy motorway. The air held the warm smell of straw. You could see for miles.

2. The footpath curves left and drops down to the hedge-line, then crosses a wooden footbridge over a ditch where a stream flows. Now turn right keeping the hedge and overgrown ditch on your right.

3. Soon you will see a house and barns on your left, partly hidden by trees. This is Housham Hall. It was a manor house in the feudal days then rebuilt with a brick facing in the 18th century. Don't take the path towards Housham Hall but cross the ditch to follow the curve of the field edge until you reach a yellow arrow sign.

Matching Church scene

Matching open space

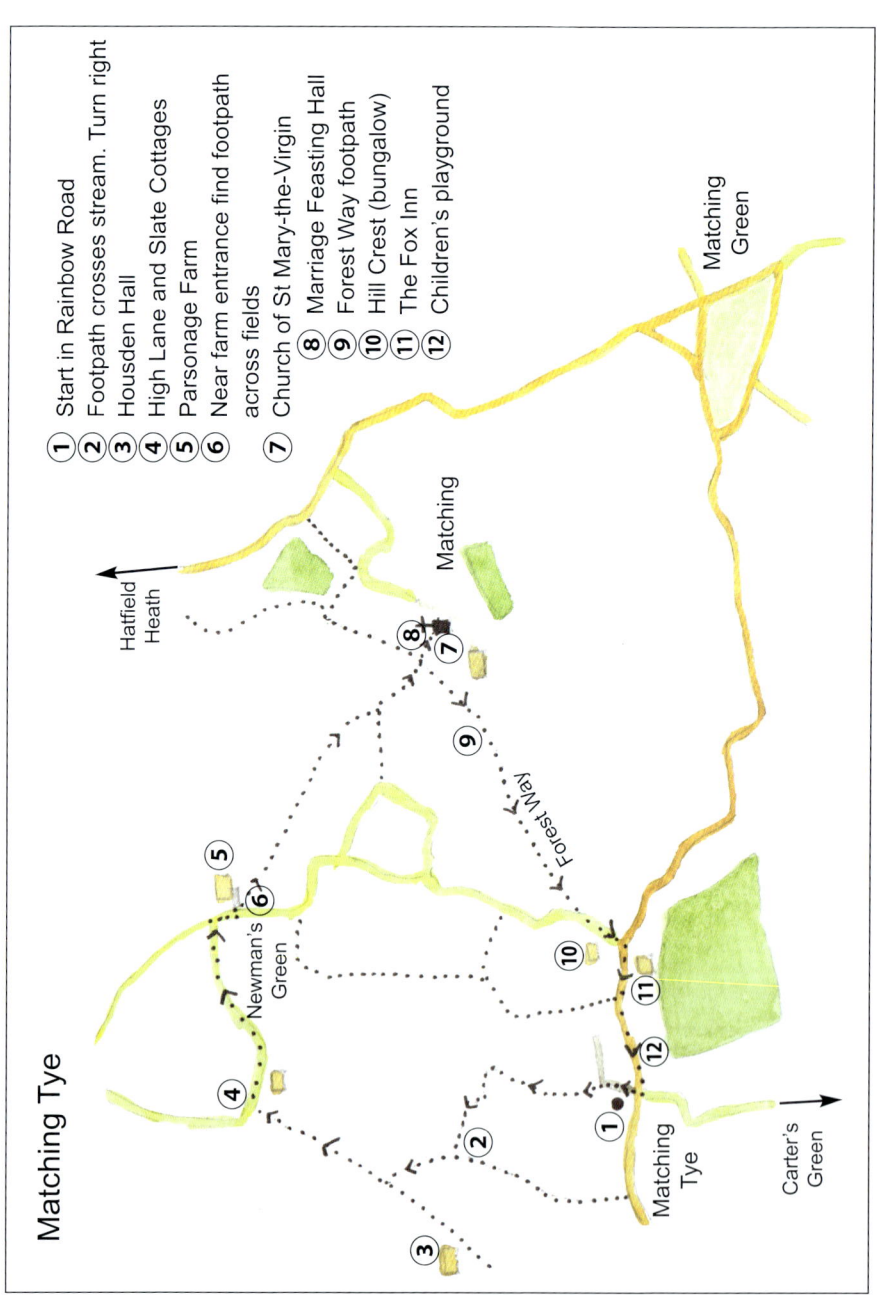

Matching Tye

4. Turn right to follow an overgrown narrow path between hedges that takes you up to a little road. (Look out for a thatched house on your right to confirm you are on track.) This is High Lane and here you turn right. Do pause to enjoy the lovely view. You pass a quaint thatched dog kennel before you come to Slate Cottages, AD 1649.

Here I found some summer-sweetened blackberries.

Keep going with hedges on both sides where the last knapweed still flower beside white yarrow and yellow cat's ears. Tall cow mumble stalks stand out from the crowd.

5. You come to Newman's Green as High Lane ends and here you turn right to find a cluster of cottages. The garden of one is a mist of pink and purple cosmos in summer. In the central green is a rusty iron pump. Turn left here to find Parsonage Farm beyond a pond edged with rushes.

Chestnut Cottage was brimming with begonias spilling from hanging baskets all along the garage wall as well as in many pots and tubs – vibrant with orange and vivid red.

6. Turn right just before the farm drive to follow the footpath that climbs gently between fields.

   Textured with dry, dusty-brown beans and blackened pods in late summer when I walked this way. Horsetail ferns – an ancient plant edged the path as it climbed gently heading straight for the tower of the church. Areas of woodland surrounded the fields on either side. On the left in the garden of a brick house a line of washing waved in the wind, trousers and sheets among other things!

7. The path brings you nearer the church before it veers to the right and another lane where the whisper of aspen trees fills the air. Here turn left and walk down towards the next footpath signs that point right along the Stort Valley Way/Forest Way – but before you continue, make a diversion to the Church of St Mary the Virgin. Now you are in Matching itself.

8. Walk up the road, passing the 1864 grey brick house on your right and ahead you will see the Tudor Marriage Feasting Hall (1480) where poor folk could celebrate their wedding days. The roof is of handmade red clay tiles. It belongs to the church but has been used as a school (1824) and

Matching Church with Tudor Hall

alms-houses in former times. Behind it stands the Norman church of flint rubble with its 15th century tower and a clock from Epping church. A magnificent oak tree (planted by Lady Selwin-Ibbeston in 1887), stands on the green where a tiny kissing gate allows you into the churchyard. The 13th century doorway leads to steps down into the nave. The church was restored by Henry Selwin Ibbetson who died in 1902. There is a window dedicated to him.

It is dark, cool and smells of old hymn books. A little sign tells me that I may take a free Bible if I am without one. How kind! On the wall is an old brass to John Ballett – a gent in 1638. The octagonal carved wooden pulpit was carefully created in 1624. I spy a pretty window dedicated to Dorothy Burton (Salmon) who used all her talents to serve this church, village and community. The clock strikes eleven. Time to move on.

9. Retrace your steps past the entrance to Matching Hall (mainly rebuilt in the 17th century) and the adjoining farm, to the Forest Way. Turn left to walk between the hedge and the field.

Early autumn is here – in the hedgerow. Arching red rosehips and black beads of elderberries, with field scabious of delicate blue flowers in the seeding grass. A walnut tree hangs over the path with wide leaves and green cases of walnuts and then you come to a crab-apple tree, branches laden with fruit. Crab apple jelly! I hear the rasping screech of a Jay – who flies ahead, disturbed by my approach. Somewhere high above a buzzard is mewing.

10. You will soon see houses ahead as you reach a road again. A bungalow called Hill Crest stands opposite – with an immaculate garden – not a blade of grass out of place! Turn left and pass the 30 mph. speed limit. Slate Cottages appear and Rose Cottage, then thatched Foxton Cottage in a garden full of colour. Next you come to Gainsborough Cottage (1692) complete with dove cote and shutters.

11. There are benches on the green and here is the Fox Inn, if you need a comfort stop. Inside there are lights twinkling in the dark windows. It sprawls along the road side and is festooned with flowers in summer.

I cross the road and step down into the heavily beamed pub. Light gleams on the bottles and glasses behind the counter as I enter the bar. Soon I am

Fox Inn, Matching

sipping a latte coffee and munching a biscuit. Collections of tiny matchbox cars are displayed around me. The Fox was first licensed in 1809. Over the years it has been extended and now includes a small hotel in its grounds. Guests are invited to stay in luxury bedrooms and tuck into a full English breakfast. Food is served every day. I read the menu chalked on a board. Spicy sausage casserole served with mashed potatoes or French onion soup. I am told that we are only twenty minutes from London for folk who fancy a stay in the country.

12. Outside with the Fox behind you turn left and walk along the busy road back towards your car. Take care – for a short stretch there is no pavement. There is a children's playground on your left. You pass a row of semi-detached houses on your right.

    In the garden of Number 6, deep, cerise-coloured dahlias caught my eye in a border edged with bright pink petunias. Someone had been busy.

    Soon you see Rainbow Road again, your starting place.

Walk 9: Stock

A delightful walk along leafy lanes including a tower mill and an ancient church as well as the village itself.

Distance	2.9 miles or 4.7 km
Time	2 hours at a gentle pace
Start	Free car parking at the village hall in Common Road
Terrain	Mainly level, one or two inclines
Map	OS Explorer 175 Southend & Basildon
Refreshments	The Dandelion & Burdock serves food Mon to Sat 9am-4pm. 01277 829772 info@dandelion-burdock.co.uk The Hoop, a weather-boarded pub serves home-cooked food; 01277 841137 www.thehoop.co.uk The local shop has sandwiches etc. for a picnic
Toilets	No public toilets on route but may be found at eateries and pubs
Getting there	Bus 100 a variable service from Chelmsford via Billericay and Basildon. Nearest railway station is Billericay. By car. Take the B1007 (once an ancient track through forests) from the A12 towards Billericay. As you enter the village of Stock take the first left turn by the Baker's Arms and park behind the village hall

1. Turn left at the entrance to the village hall and walk along Common Road. You pass Birch Lane before you come to Mill Walk. Here you turn left on St Peter's Way. The Nook confirms your route. At a private drive take the right fork to follow path to a housing estate, keep to the path, bearing right into a wide, grassy stretch. You will reach Mill Lane.

2. Time for a detour! Turn left and walk about 100 yards to see Stock Windmill built of soft red brick. In summer months it is open in the

Stock sign

Stock windmill

afternoon on the second Sunday of the month. Free admission but donations most welcome.

When I did this walk I was able to see inside the mill and climb the narrow wooden stairs right to the seven ton cap at the top which turns on an iron track in the wind. Beneath what seemed like an upturned boat that creaked as the fantail moved, I stared at the great wheels with wooden teeth above my head. From tiny windows, beyond the white sails, were rooftops and woodland. It was used to grind flour for meal and cattle cake from 1816 until 1936. For some years Mary Clover was the miller. The ¾ ton stones were imported from France and installed in sections.

3. Retrace your steps along Mill Lane to a T-junction where you turn left into Mill Road. Take care, there is no pavement and it can be busy. Walk along this tree-lined stretch with neat hedges defining gardens where in early summer wisteria crawls over walls and rhododendrons create splashes of bold orange and pink. Pass Yew Tree Cottage (left) and Mill Cottage (right). Opposite the gates at Stockwell House (of honey-coloured bricks) is a footpath sign pointing right into the wood.

4. Go under a sycamore tree into a dry ditch to follow a narrow path between hedges and fences.

   I shuffled through brown leaf litter. A blackbird sang from an overgrown garden. Jack-by-the-hedge flowers, buttercups and nettles edged the way. Horses grazed in a paddock to my right. Then came a pebbledash wall and suddenly a little road appeared.

5. Turn left to pass Siljan down a neglected driveway.

   Now turn right into Madles Lane where you will pass the oldest, continually inhabited house in Stock; Broadmoor Cottage dated 1490. A footpath goes beside it, but not the one we're taking. Continue along the leafy lane where towering oaks stretch out their branches and forget-me-nots and red campion flower in late spring amidst a froth of white cow parsley.

   Broadmore Cottage

6. On the left you will see Thrift – a German kit house, constructed in only a few weeks. It offers an intriguing insight!

   Look out for Scrivener's Farm beyond iron gates. Once a dilapidated house it has been completely rebuilt.

7. Turn right into Marigold Lane.

   An old hedge-cutter once said to a stranger, "Nothing ever grows here 'cept marigolds".

   The stranger later built a house and called it Marigolds.

   The grey tarmacked lane curves to pass The Hawthorns before it drops to a T-junction.

8. Cross the road to follow a track over a stream.

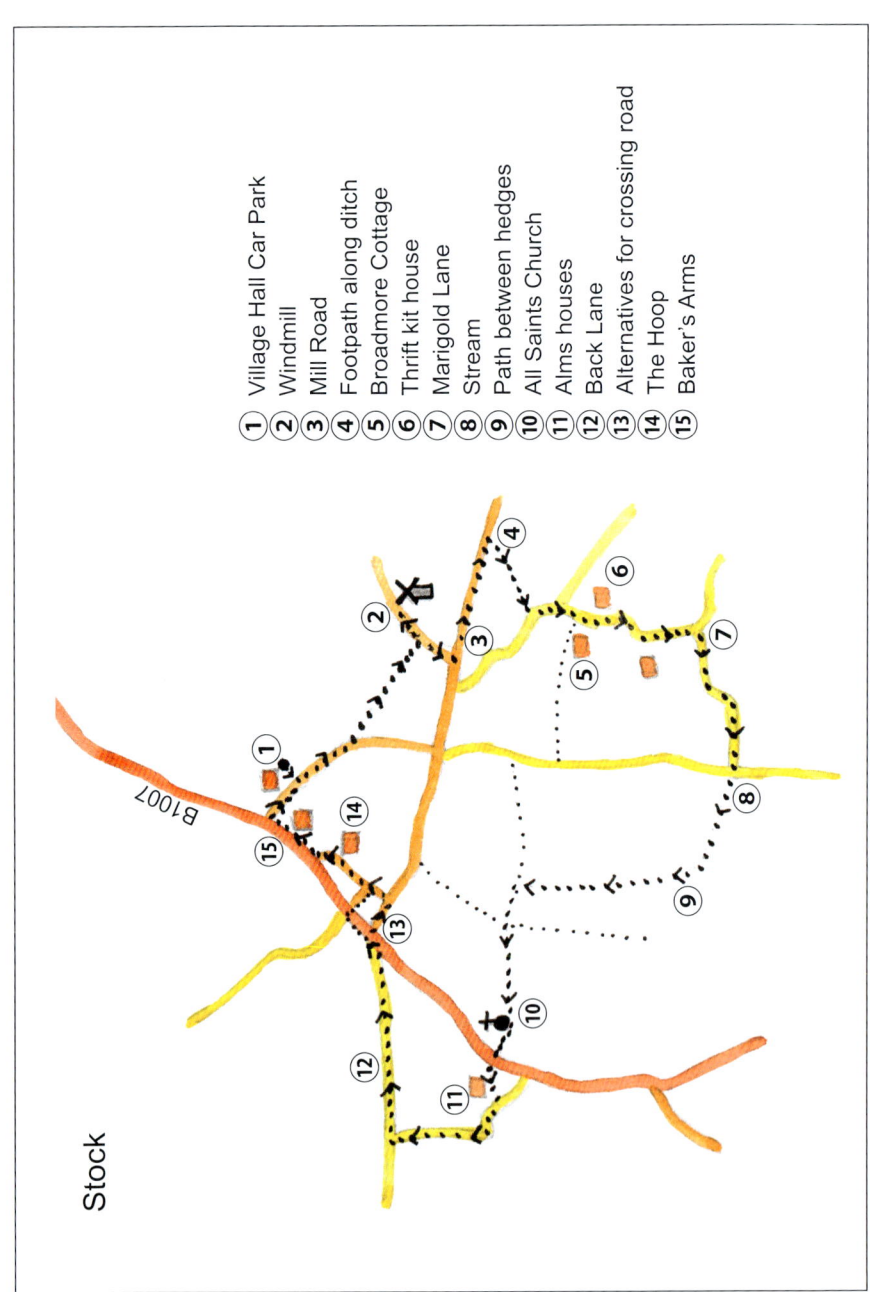

There was no visible footpath sign but an old stile indicates the way.

Look out for Pilgrims Farm where a white iron seat encircles a tree. The footpath has a slight incline here.

Furry chocolate brown alpacas nibbled grass in a field where buttercups gleamed. They ignored me as I walked by.

9. At a pond (on the left) turn right to walk up a grassy path between mixed hedges where wild roses bloom in early summer alongside the white flowers of the wayfaring tree and the guelder rose. Peep over the hedge to see young sweet chestnuts planted in neat rows. Soon the path enters woodland and grass is replaced by compressed soil as you walk through a tunnel of blackthorn trees.

Squeeze through the gap by a stile and find a yellow arrow. Turn left opposite a high fence. Look for strange contorted tree shapes where someone once pollarded the hornbeams. Here is an ancient bank, once part of the boundary line that encircled Stock. You reach a kissing gate. Over the fence to your right Roman pottery has been found.

Across the field a greater spotted woodpecker hammered at a telegraph pole. A magpie hopped across the grass and an unseen chiff-chaff called his repetitive notes.

Another yellow arrow directs you left to a gateway where you turn right. The path drops to a wooden footbridge over a dry ditch then takes a steep upward slope to pass some stables on your left.

10. Now you come to All Saints Churchyard which is a good place for a picnic as there are several benches here. As you walk beside the headstones pause to read of vivacious Ronald George Yates and Derek John Puddifant. Find the Asplin family graves and that of Sir Vernon Harry Stuart Haggard, JP, who has a memorial in the church.

The Garden of Remembrance (1953) marks the spot where a land mine fell on December 13th 1940. It destroyed the nave roof and shattered the stained glass. It shook the very foundations of the tower and unhinged the bells. But the early Norman walls on the south and west of the nave survived, probably because they're one metre thick in places. The church was restored by 1981. At the top of its shingled spire is a fine dragon weather vane.

I wandered around the building to see the pudding stones – embedded rounded pebbles used for building and the thin Roman bricks here and there in the oldest remaining walls. Near the 1683 wooden bell tower a pouting face with podgy cheeks stares down from above. The door was unlocked so I stepped down into the coolness of the church. White and red Tudor roses decorated the roof and a Bible lay open at Isaiah 61 on the eagle lectern. In the nave is a brass to Richard Twedy, 1574, who built the alms-houses opposite the church.

11. As you leave the church cross the busy road to find a gravel track opposite Bellman's Farm. You will see the old pump on your left. By the quaint alms-houses turn right, near a copper beech tree, into St Peter's Way again. This is School Lane, indeed the old school is just over the hedge.

Stock church

Bellman's Farmhouse

12. The lane curves (take care) and takes you beside farmland beneath more huge oak trees. You will see Foster's Close where children played when I was here and then comes a T-junction where you turn right onto Back Lane.

    This *was once the salt road from Maldon to Ongar. Long ago salt was used as currency.*

    Now there are bungalows and new builds on either side as you head back into Stock.

    Pass Dakyn Drive on your left then The Cottage on your right. Note that several other pretty cottages are named after flowers. See how many you can find. You will notice the sound of the traffic as you draw nearer the road.

13. Cross carefully at Saddlers opposite the Wines and Spirit Store to pass The Bear Inn on your right. Or, if the road is busy, walk past the Harvard Inn on your left to take the pedestrian crossing by the village store, a safer option.

    This is the High Street and here you will find Dandelion and Burdock if you need some refreshment. Turn left to walk parallel to the main road passing a terrace of Victorian cottages on your right. Across the road are weather-boarded Ellis Cottages.

    Ellis Cottages

14. Look for The Coach House (not so long ago the doctor's surgery), then pass the War Memorial before you come to The Hoop. In 1460 it was three weaver's cottages, then in the early 1900s became an ale house. Inside are sturdy timbers once used in ship building. Wagons from Tilbury docks transported them inland.

15. At The Baker's Arms (another stopping place) turn right into Common Road. You are almost back to the start by the village hall.

Walk 10: Blackmore End

This is an easy walk on fairly level ground with no stiles. It skirts field boundaries and follows country lanes, with one short section on a busy road. It begins and ends in the heart of the village.

Distance	3 miles or 4.9 km
Time	1½ hours
Start	Park by the village green
Terrain	Level but for one upward incline
Map	OS Explorer 195 Braintree & Saffron Walden
Refreshments	None in Blackmore End. The village green is a good place for a picnic. See page 168 for nearby Great Bardfield.
Toilets	No public toilets
Getting there	Take the A1071 from Braintree to Hedingham. The roads to Wethersfield (either at Gosfield or Sible Hedingham) go towards Blackmore End. Look out for signposts before you reach Wethersfield itself. There are no regular buses

Blackmore End had a population of four hundred and fifty souls in 1348. In 1349 when the Black Death came calling, the population was reduced to about one hundred and fifty. Travellers sought to avoid the village and lanes were created to by-pass it, one is called Red Rose Lane because of the red skin blemishes that signalled plague.

It was a beautiful morning in early spring. Daffodils were just thinking about opening to herald the coming of warmer days. Birdsong resonated from hedgerows and trees and the grass was showing a vibrant green. Pretty cottages looked over the Village Green where three roads converged and here I parked my car.

The narrow lane Blackmore End

1. Start at the central green where a stream flows gently by the roadside and two cottages, The Smithy and Daisy Cottage (with patterned pargetting), give a backdrop as pretty as a picture. At the main road turn left, opposite a thatched cottage. Cross the stream and head up the hill away from the village. You will see Brook Cottage on your right then Owl's Hall Farm.

2. With another grassy space on the left and Thatched Cottage behind a picket fence you come to a track and a byway sign beside the cottage, here you leave the road. A red doggy bin marks the way! This is Hyde Lane – a well-trodden footpath. The hedge is thick – mainly hawthorn and ivy and young oak trees. Look out for barns on the right, beyond a grassy paddock. Soon you reach the road.

   Among the woodland that edged the track were clumps of snowdrops and bright yellow aconites.

3. Time for a detour. Turn left to tramp along this quiet little road. You will see an oast house on your right.

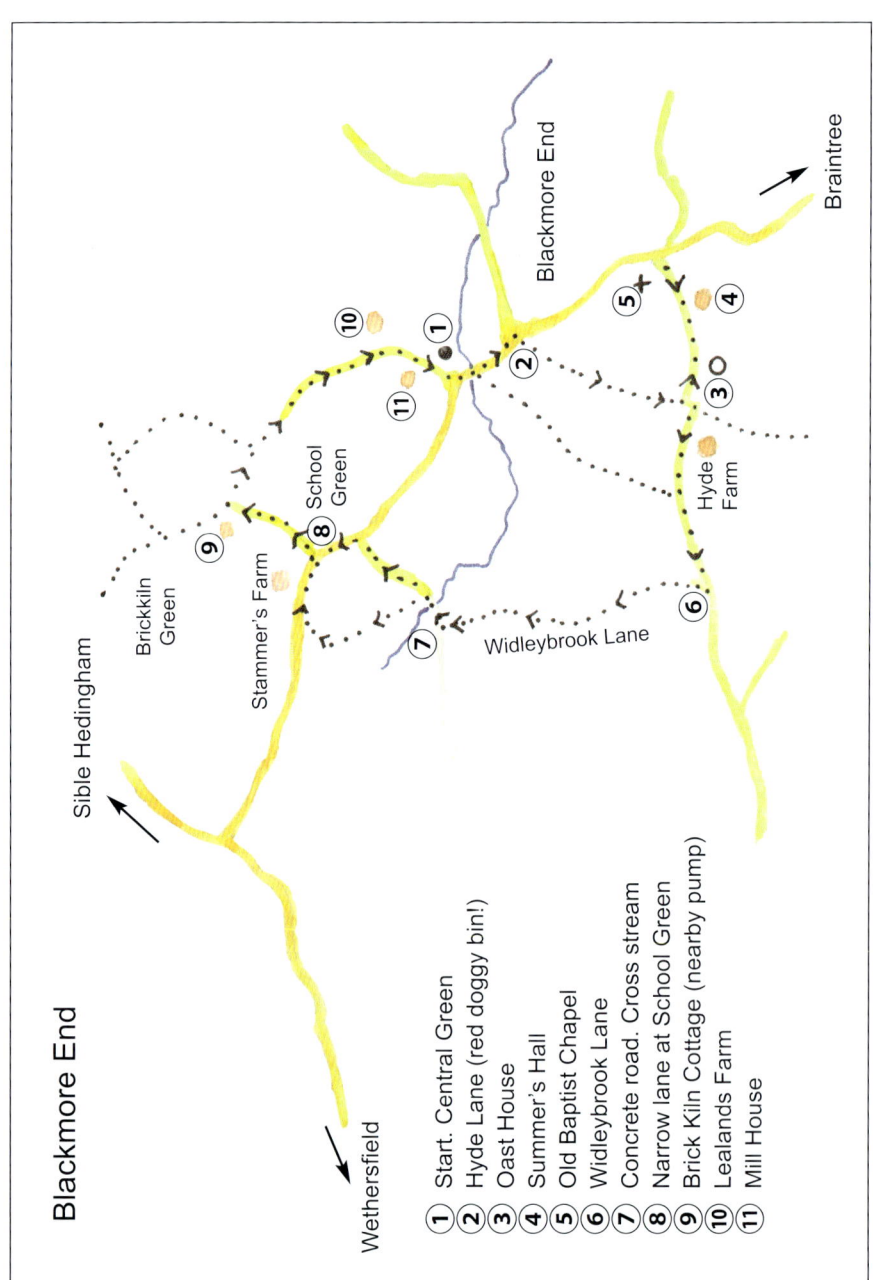

The owner told me that this is in fact a folly, built in the 1970s. The land once belonged to Julien Courtauld who lived next door. He said that you can only access the oast house by ladders. Now I am curious to see the house next door!

4. Barns and outbuildings indicate 15th century Summers Hall – set back beyond a gravelled drive and a turning circle. It is a long, sprawling, timber-framed manor house with a two gables under a slate and handmade clay tile roof.

   This is Julian Courtauld's home. He was born 1938, a member of the Courtauld family who in 1794 were the world's leading man-made fibre production company. They started in Pebmarsh with a silk textile business. Three mills were built in nearby Halstead and Braintree and in 1850 about 2,000 workers (mainly women) were employed there. Because of their Calvanistic background the family believed they owed a debt to the community and so set up charitable trusts to plough back some of the profits. In Braintree is the William Julien Courtauld Hospital and in 1912 a yacht was built called 'Duet'. The Duet Fund offers young people opportunities to experience sailing adventures.

   Summer's Hall

5. A little further along the road is the 1843 red brick Baptist chapel with a strange sign on the gate 'Beware of the Dog.' But there is a second gate and here you can wander into the cemetery and find the headstones, some leaning against the church wall. Read the names; Basil Edward Terry and Frank Stock – only five months old, among others. If you hadn't guessed it – the church is now a private home.

   Retrace your footsteps back to the road and indeed back to where you left Hyde Lane. Now you turn right, along the narrow lane passing Hyde Farm with a pond and restored barns where unseen terriers bark.

6. You will pass 'Betelgeuse' and see wide open fields bordered by brambles. Look for a public Bridleway sign on the right, half hidden in a hedge. Here you leave the road again with a house to your left and some horizontal thick wooden poles. The muddy track leads past a dilapidated old shepherds hut

on wheels and a tiny thatched house on your right.

This is Widleybrook Lane. Now you are heading into open countryside with woodland and farmland. Wooden pylons carry electricity wires across the field. This by-way bears left, but you continue straight on, following rutted tyre-tracks by the hedge line. The path gently falls until you come to a T-junction.

Blackmore End fields

7. Turn right onto a concrete road where puddles collect on rainy days. Cross a stream and then veer left to tramp up the hill towards more houses. There is a thick hedge on both sides to shelter you from the wind. You will pass a paddock.

When I walked this way, shaggy donkeys were grazing. They lifted their heads to watch me. On their fence the sign said 'Private No Parking'.

You soon reach the main road. Before you cross, do turn to look back over the landscape and you will be rewarded by faraway views.

8. This is a busy road and there is no pavement, though the grass verge provides relative safety from traffic. It is only a short stretch but do take care. You will see a low thatched cottage ahead. This is School Green Cottage, painted pink. Turn right into a narrow lane. Look out for a VR postbox. Stay on this road, ignoring a footpath sign pointing right. In spring purple violets cluster among the young nettles by the roadside. You come to other pretty cottages, some with peg-tiled roofs, others thatched.

9. At Brick-Kiln cottage where daffodils herald spring, find a track bearing right into

Blackmore End cottage

Oast House

woodland. Here is an old iron pump, a clue to former days. It has a wooden structure supporting it. I wonder when it was last used. This footpath may be muddy (it is well used by horses, judging by the hoof-prints), follow it between trees until you reach Rosemary Cottage on your left. Here bear right with the track which takes you to Lower Green Farm.

10. Look out for a little, yellow oast house with a central chimney pot poking out from its grey thatch.

Continue on passing a pond with a central island of a willow tree. This is by a house called Wrights. It has a gable on one end. Lealands Barn and farm come next and now you are not far from your starting place. Mill House stands back on your right. Then comes Thanet House where you can buy free range eggs. As you see the central green appear look for The Smithy, a lovely little weather-boarded cottage behind a picket fence.

In spring the window boxes were vibrant with colour; purple and yellow crocus proclaimed the season. Daffodils peeped though the upright fence post creating a lovely picture.

Mill House

In 1851, a Thomas Smee was licenced to sell alcohol here and it remained open until 2010. A developer bought it with the idea of converting it into a house but there was an outcry from the locals who opposed the planning application. It was rejected. The villagers raised money to buy it and offered him £30.000 but he said no. However two years later a local couple bought it and it has been renovated and restored. Today it serves lunches from Tuesday to Sunday and offers a take-away menu too. In 2016 the Bull was the winner of The Diner's Choice Open Table Award. Sadly in recent days loss of trade has closed The Bull, the last of five pubs in the village.

I arrive too early for the lunch-time food, but the manager, kindly makes me a frothy coffee served in a tall glass. The Bull has been thoughtfully refurbished throughout and there is plenty of space to eat outside on a sunny day. Julia tells me that it is popular with local people. The menu offers wild mushroom and tarragon risotto and beer-battered fish and chips.

I return to my car down on the village green, a good place to have a picnic. It's time to head for home.

Walk 11: High Roding to Great Canfield

Amidst lovely countryside not far from Great Dunmow is High Roding and its tiny neighbour Great Canfield.

Distance	Approximately 3.1 miles or 5 km. A circular walk along country lanes and through Essex farmland
Time	About 2 hours at a gentle pace
Start	Free car park behind the Old School in the main street of High Roding
Terrain	No steep climbs but gradual ups-and-downs
Map	OS Explorer 183 Chelmsford & The Rodings
Refreshments	The Black Lion is open seven days a week and has a varied menu. 01371 872847 www.theblacklionhighroding.co.uk
Toilets	No public toilets on route
Getting there	By car take the B184 from Great Dunmow (a fine Roman road) a mile or so to High Roding. You pass the Tea Rooms as you look for the blue 'P' sign further into the village. The 17 and 18 bus service runs from Chelmsford to Dunmow on Tuesdays and Thursdays

As I left my car I saw a yellow arrow beneath a hawthorn tree in the corner of the car park. It pointed into lovely countryside. I checked my map, the sun came out and a sky lark began to sing – a good way to start my walk.

1. From the car park follow the field edge, heading towards Great Canfield keeping the ditch to your right.

   When you reach a footbridge turn right, keeping to a field edge now with the ditch on your left.

High Roding fields

> *Creamy white blossom adorned the hedge and bright stars of celandine shone from the grassy verge. Yellow lichen was daubed along the branches on the trees.*

2. Ignore a footpath sign on your left and stride out across the open field as it gradually rises towards the road. Watch out for another footpath (left) that cuts straight down the field, running parallel to the road. The farmer has marked the route through his crop. Here is a wonderful sense of space. Ahead is the extensive tree-clad castle mound and to the right you will see a red-bricked house. The path drops to the stream where you find another footbridge. Keep going to *another* wooden footbridge and follow the hedge-line by a cottage garden. There are apple trees on your left.

3. Go straight across the garden to a thick hedge where you'll find a narrow opening onto the road. Here you turn left to reach Great Canfield. Soon you'll see the church peeping out from the trees to your left. A little river flows beneath the road and the castle mound is closer now, rising up to your left.

> *A chalked blackboard stood by the road side at Bury Farm Cottages saying, 'Beef for Sale'. The sound of a mower in someone's garden spoke of summer, together with the sweet fragrance of newly cut grass.*

4. Turn left at a footpath sign to walk by a fence, along a field edge towards the church. Cross a narrow concrete bridge over a stream, ducking under the branches of an elder tree.

5. Here is the Norman church of St Mary the Virgin with its wooden spire.

   I wandered across the grass spotted with daisies and blue speedwell flowers, passing the headstone to Gwendoline Goddard, wife, mother, granny and great granny. 1911-2009. She almost made one hundred. Sadly the door was locked but if you telephone 01279 870620 David will come and let you in – a sign tells me.

6. Beyond the wide lych-gate where spent flowers are discarded in a plastic box are some pretty tiled cottages. Walk onto the little road to survey the rural scene. There are patterned tiles on the roof too. Look for a footpath sign on the left by Rose Cottage. This takes you by the wooden fence of The Hall towards barns. There is a yellow arrow on a telegraph post. Turn right at the end of the garden and walk over rough ground passing a log pile. Wooden crates are stacked high to your left, bearing NAISH and WHK – whatever that means!

7. The path creeps behind the farm buildings, circling the hall. You walk by tractors, trailers and a muck heap bearing left to find a yellow arrow by a ditch. Now you find yourself in lovely countryside. Through the hedge on your left you glimpse rolling stock, ploughs and harrows, stacked-up tractor tyres and yet more tractors. To your right are lovely faraway views. Walk down the field edge to a wooden footbridge. Turn right walk to the corner of the field where you bear left and left again. As you enter another field bear right. Look out for a faded yellow arrow to confirm you are on track. The stream (choked with rushes) will be on your left.

8. You come to a river where willow trees grow and here you cross another bridge.

   There was a trickling sound of water and a wood-pigeon cooed where the willow stretched out its branches. I paused on the bridge to enjoy the sense of peace in this delightful spot and watch the river rippling beneath me. All around were open fields and the sun was warm. Primroses and purple violets fought for space amidst the ground ivy. I looked back to see Hall Farm.

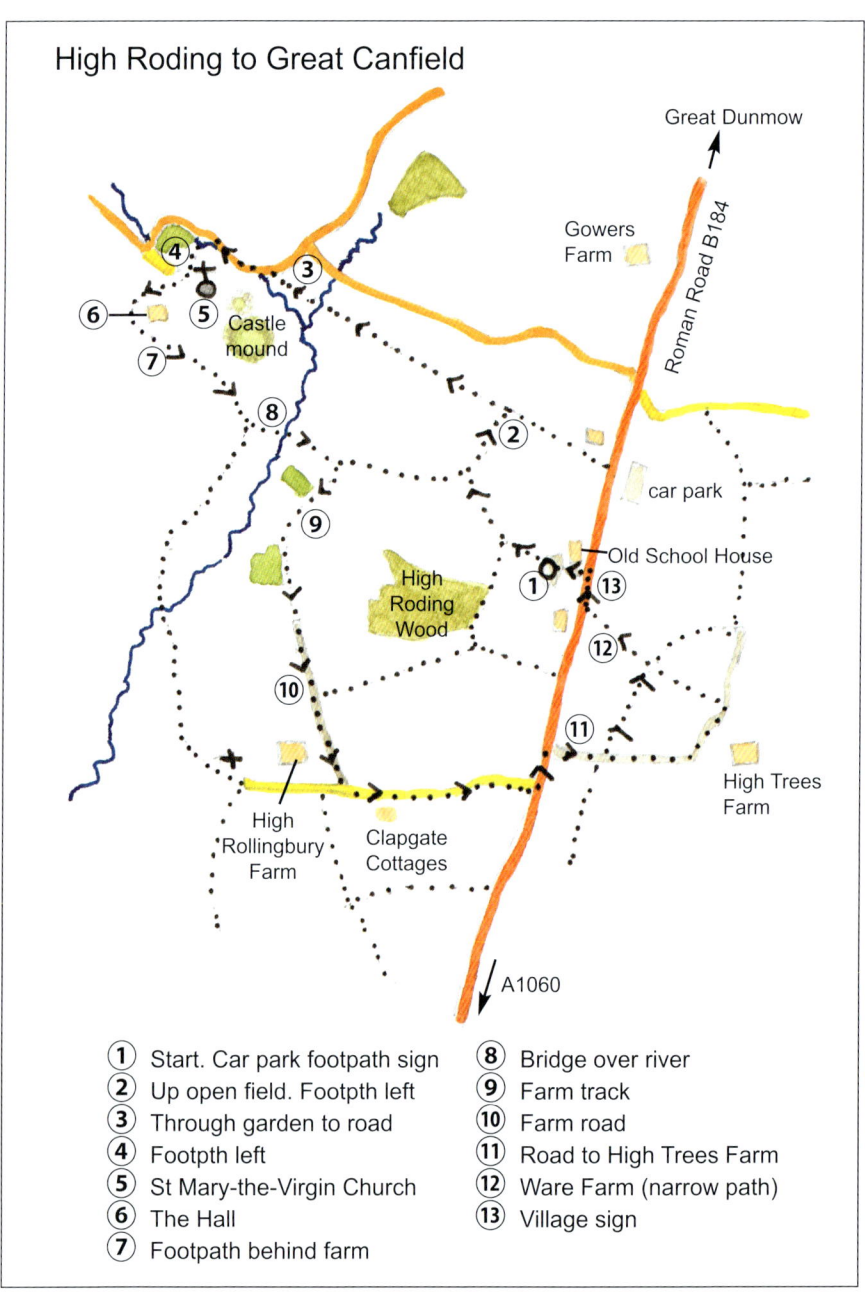

Walk along the upper edge of a field with a patch of woodland to your right. There are feeding stations for pheasants. In spring cowslips flower along the verges. You come to a neatly clipped hedge on your left and here you bear left towards more woodland.

9. You will see High Rodingbury Wood to your left across the field beyond a deep ditch. The footpath becomes a wider track and begins to climb. Go straight on, keeping a white farmhouse to your right. Look too for a black weather-boarded barn. Then you come to an open barn where hay is stacked to the roof and trailers stand.

10. On your right is a tangle of old machinery, corrugated tin and brambles as you reach a farm road. Here is High Rodingbury Farm. Turn left onto the farm road

High Rodingbury Farm

High Roding Church

Black Lion

where (in April) more primroses flower in the wide grass verges.

If you turn right here – you can make a detour to visit another country church. The sun was hot so I kept going towards my stopping place. Red tulips added colour at Clapgate Cottages on my right and I reach the 40 mph sign. A chiff-chaff called and a yellow brimstone butterfly drifted across my path.

Thatch Roof High Roding.

11. You come to a busy road which you need to cross to take the road to High Trees Farm. You will pass the sewage works where the final effluent sample gushes from a pipe. Just beyond this take a footpath to your left. There are farm buildings on your right.

12. Take another left footpath up a field edge keeping the hedge to your left to the backs of houses where, when I walked, washing was blowing in the breeze and dustbins and water butts stood side by side. You will soon be back in the village. Nearly there. The path narrows between the barn of Ware Farm and a high fence. It brings you back onto the main road through High Roding. Turn right.

If you look left there is the 14th century Black Lion where food is served every day at lunch time and in the evening.

13. Walk by The Smithy and The Forge to see a delightful thatch of Crabtree Cottage where a dog and cat prance along the ridge. When you see the village sign cross the road to the Old School with its bell turret and here is your starting place.

Walk 12: Stisted

This walk in Stisted, a village nestling in the river valley not far from Braintree, includes a golf course; a meandering river; fields; country roads and the village itself. But above all (literally) are the chimneys! Just wait and see! It was also the home of Andrew Motion, poet laureate from 1999-2009. He founded The Poetry Archive. He moved here aged 12 and stayed until he went to college in Oxford. But term times were spent at boarding school so he had no friends in the village. He took to walking with his dog and here a love of the countryside became firmly established. We may well walk in his footsteps as we explore Stisted and its countryside.

Distance	3.2 miles or 5.1 km
Time	1½ hours
Start	The Onley in the village centre
Terrain	Some steep slopes down to the river valley and back
Map	OS Explorer 195 Braintree & Saffron Walden
Refreshments	The Deli café at The Onley serves breakfast and lunch every day until 2.30pm. 01376 325325 info@theonley.com Booking advisable. Benches along route in village or sit by the river for a picnic
Toilets	The Onley has top notch loos – with airblade driers!
Getting there	Look for a turning between Coggeshall and Braintree on the A120 a Roman Road. Alternatively the A1017 from Hedingham to Braintree brings you here. There is a bus from Braintree on Wednesdays

1. Park outside The Onley (named after Mr Saville Onley of Stisted Hall), a newly refurbished red brick pub in the centre of the village. It stands on the site of the Black Lion – which burnt down in the early 19th century. The first landlord was Albert Earle – who had a blacksmith's forge close by. Locals speak of a huge chestnut tree that once grew just outside.

With The Onley behind you turn right and walk down the hill towards the church, passing pretty cottages with bressumers of carved foliage and elaborately decorated chimneys. At the bend in the road take a concreted drive by the village notice board where a sign announces 'Bells are rung regularly at this church'.

2. The buttressed wall is the boundary of the churchyard and here you will find the lych-gate, adorned with white bird's droppings!

From somewhere nearby came the sound of young children's voices, a cacophony of shouting, squealing and crying. Someone wants their mum! The blue church clock says 10.20. I am on a quest to find the headstones of Andrew Motion's parents, buried just beyond the church tower. Catherine Gillian Motion, died in 1978 and Andrew Richard Motion T.D. died in 2006. I linger to read the inscription.

> 'The wonder of the world, the beauty and the power.
> The shapes of things, their colours, lights, shades.
> These I saw. Look ye also, while life lasts'.

All Saints Church, Stisted

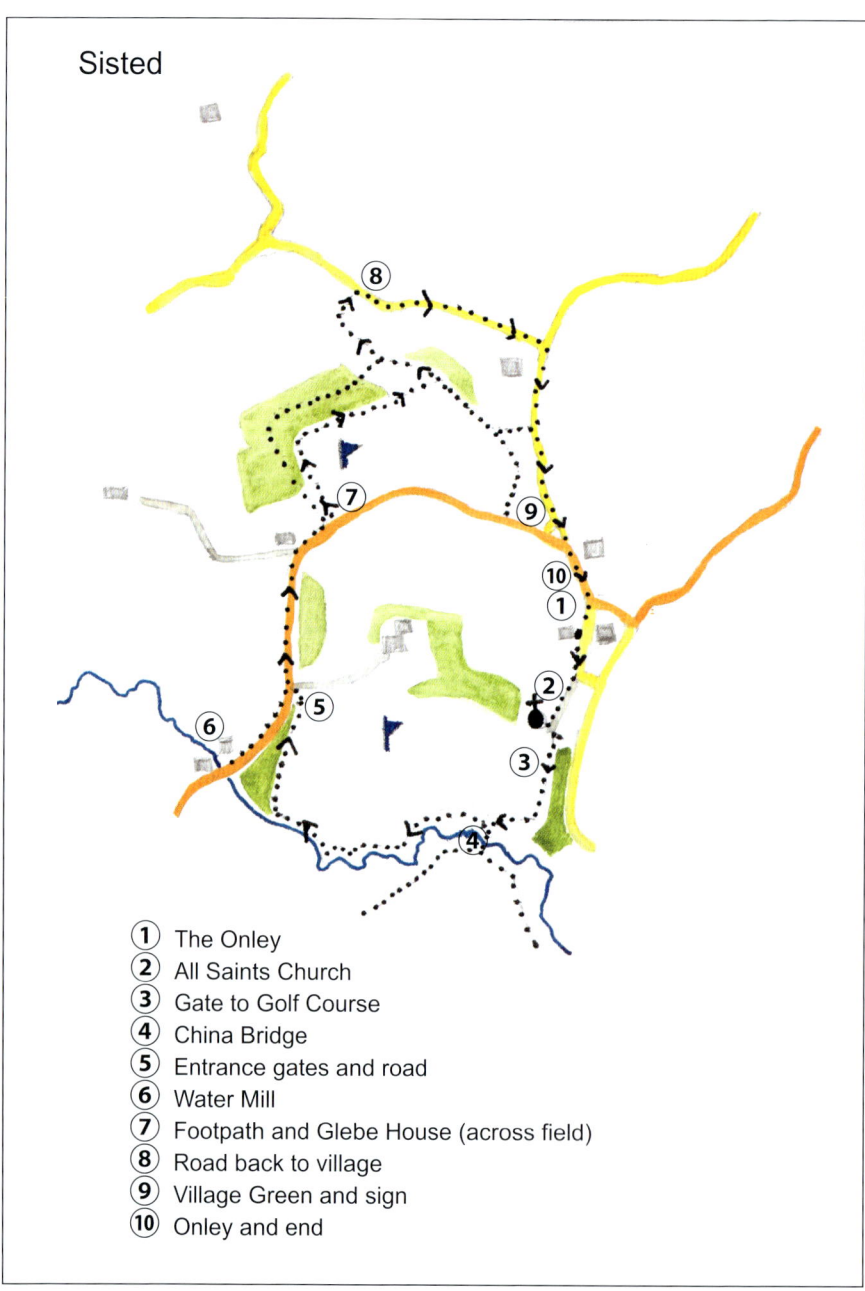

Sadly eight hundred year old All Saints Church is locked. I had hoped to see a painting by Gaspar de Crayer called 'The Adoration of the Magi'. It was given to the church by the great-grandparents of Andrew Motion. It is a copy of a Rubens hung in King's College Cambridge.

3. Take time to explore the churchyard to look for the grave of the builder of the wonderful chimneys before you pass the pollarded lime trees to continue your stroll. Turn right and head for a kissing gate, in the shadow of a huge spreading chestnut tree adorned with white candle flowers in May. Here is the golf course. The public are warned of the dangers of flying golf balls. We are ordered to keep strictly to the footpath and go without delay!

An arrow points to the footpath with the fairway on your right and tall trees on your left. You come to a curve at the lower end of the grass where in May thick clumps of purple comfrey flowers are alive with bees. Look for a pathway to make a short detour to the river Blackwater which winds its way through the valley.

4. Here is China Bridge.

I stood on the bridge and peered down into the flowing water where the submerged reeds were bending in the mysterious depths. Inky black and purple damsel flies flittered above the surface and a dragonfly zinged past.

Return to the fairway to walk with the river on your left. Keep watching out for low-flying golf balls! We are in Stisted Park, the honey-coloured house can be seen through gaps in the trees and shrubs. The river bank tall trees offer shade from the sun; huge aspens with hollow-stemmed leaves that tremble in the faintest breeze and grey-leaved willows. You will soon pass Hole 15. Nearby is an old oak tree. You will hear running water as you come to a weir with various signs; 'No Swimming. Danger of Diving'. Ignore a wooden footbridge.

5. Keeping the trees on your left with their verge of nettles, climb the slope by the golf course as it curves upward and away from the river. Yellow arrows confirm the footpath. Soon you will come to the entrance gates and the road. Here is another sign. No Public Right of Way but look for the footpath sign half hidden in the hedgerow that does indeed point clearly to the route you have just walked.

6. Watch out for traffic here – the painted white lines signal that this is quite a busy road. As a detour head down the hill to the river to see the white weather-boarded mill by the sun-warmed bricks of the bridge. A mill has been on this spot since the 11th century and this one could be four hundred years old. The roof was caving in when the Millers bought it in 1976. They have carefully restored it.

Here was a field golden with buttercups – a lovely scene with the flowing water edged by tall yellow irises and trailing willow branches. The sunshine danced on the water reflecting the blue of the sky. I tramped back up the steep hill, passing Mill House with an open front door.

From the entrance to the golf course follow the road enjoying the views to your left. Ahead you will see Covenbrook Hall Cottages as pretty as a picture. Here the road curves right and brings you to a choice of footpaths on the left. One goes through woodland and close by it the second skirts the golf course again. They bring you out in the same place.

I chose the path by the golf course and followed its boundary. From the woodland on my left came exuberant birdsong and the oniony smell of ransomes. The thwack of a golf club alerted me to the presence of some

elderly men wearing caps, shorts, white socks and plimsolls and pushing their buggies as a mother would push her precious child. One man looked in our direction, scowled and turned away. Perhaps walkers are not welcome? A few minutes later a flying golf ball cracked into a tree and bounced down into the grass. A close encounter!

7. When you reach pine trees whose cones litter the path, find a footpath (left) that takes you into a field where an elegant white house gleams against the trees that surround it. This is Glebe House, the home of Andrew Motion for 6 years. Follow the field edge keeping a ditch on your left until you pass an oak tree on your right. Here you will see a gap in the hedge and a broken fence post. Keep going forward with a paddock to your right. Ignore a wooden footbridge over the dry ditch full of old brown leaves and pass by another paddock then follow the path left, ducking under low branches to find yourself in an open field surrounded by lovely views. Faraway is Braintree but before you is a field stretching to the horizon and when I walked here a blue sky dotted with cotton wool clouds. With brambles on your right bear right and you will soon come to the road by another footpath sign that is covered with splodges of lichen.

Glebe House

8. Turn right to walk back to Stisted.

Across the valley to your left you will see the roof and chimney stack of Kentish's Farm beyond another paddock where a white horse lifted his head to watch me pass. Everywhere is the warm smell of horses!

Now the road with hedges either side and a line of telegraph poles, takes you back to the village. You will pass a collection of ramshackle barns to your right.

An estate agents sign informed me that these barns are 'For Sale'. As I looked at the gaps in the wooden wall where planks had come askew and hung precariously at various angles I wondered if some adventurous soul might take up the challenge. The sun was growing hotter by the minute – reflected up from the hard surface of the road as I plodded along, thinking of The Onley and a cool drink.

Pass the entrance to Glebe House then see rooftops ahead and those wonderful chimneys again. Then comes Waterlea Cottage (1692) and a 30 mph. sign. Opposite the village hall is the community orchard, allotments and wild life area. Inside the gateway are neat rows of bean sticks, sheds, poly-tunnels and several folk busy at work.

9. Now you are back to the village where a welcome green painted bench encircles a beech tree and offers a rest for the weary and shelter from hot sun. On the nearby village sign are hops – that once grew here. Look at the signpost with an absurdly long arm to one side bearing lengthy place names of nearby villages.

Stisted signpost

Stisted street

As I rest my legs a lady collects her newspaper from a box on her cottage gate and calls good morning.

Continue your walk along the street passing flint cottages with arched windows. Bear right opposite the pebble-dashed Montefiore Institution. This building was given to Stisted by the family of that name and today houses the village shop and Post Office (open six hours a week on Monday and Thursday afternoons); a room for meetings where the WI gather.

From across the street a cheerful window cleaner hails me and tells me that he lives there, upstairs. "It's lovely in the summer but jolly cold in the winter." he says. "Once it had public baths. It became a brothel as well as a reading room."

10. Now you are back to The Onley and the end of your walk.

I am soon tucking into a goat's cheese and onion marmalade sandwich in the patio area. The menu tempts me with ginger sticky-toffee pudding. The waitress tells me that The Onley re-opened in June 2016 after a complete overhaul by an enterprising business man who lives in Barbados. She also said that somewhere in the churchyard is the grave of the man who built the chimneys. I wonder where?

Walk 13: Tollesbury

Take some sea air in this bracing walk.

Distance	3.2 miles or 5.2 km
Time	2 hours
Start	Free car park. Go through village and head for the sea. As you approach the Marina and industrial units you will see the car park on the right
Terrain	Flat walking over all
Map	OS Explorer 184 Colchester, Harwich & Clacton on Sea
Refreshments	The Loft 01621 869063 thelofttearoom@gmail.com serving take-aways from Friday to Sunday 11am-3pm. Tollesbury café. 01621 869980 Winter times 9am-3pm. Opens at 10am on Sunday. Some lovely spots for a picnic on route; well-placed benches overlooking salt marshes
Toilets	In the places above and public toilets in the car park
Getting there	At Tiptree take the B1023 to Tolleshunt Knights, then Tolleshunt D'Arcy to Tollesbury. Here pass the school and take the left turn towards the Marina. Hedingham Buses run 50 and 50A services from Colchester. No train

1. Leave your car where there are public toilets and a handy bench to change into walking boots. Walk across the stretch of grass following a line of sycamore trees towards the salt marshes and estuary. The pavement here is uneven as you pass industrial units and a café before you reach the Sailing Club founded in 1936. Opposite is a sail-maker's loft.

Sail lofts

Some boats stood outside and through an open door above me I could see a figure at work. He paused to call good morning but said he had a deadline to meet. Prolonged conversation was not on his schedule.

2. You come to Woodrolfe Hard with the sea defences, sturdy gates that can be closed where the road creeps towards the estuary or the water creeps toward the road! Here you see the sailing lofts of painted wood, raised on concrete stilts where all things nautical are stored and sails are made. Ladders lean here and there to offer access to the upper floors. One has become a café if you need some refreshment.

   Take the raised pathway along the sea wall with flats on the right and a tangle of wild flowers on the bank to your left.

3. You will see Woodup Pool where families congregate to paddle and picnic, splash and swim in the murky water. A few more steps takes you to Harbour View and the Marina, jam-packed with moored boats creating a picture such as seen in a **very** hard jigsaw puzzle. The footpath goes on around the sea wall for some miles if you'd like a longer walk but for my walk retrace your steps to Woodrolfe Hard. Look out for Fellowship Afloat near the sea.

   I could not resist a quick paddle in Woodup Pool as it was a warm morning and the water looked so tempting. The soft sea weed wrapped its silky fronds around my ankles and I thought of crabs.

4. Cross the road and take the raised path along the sea wall away from the village. On your left is the Sailing Club and on the right an assortment of boats with masts furled and clinking ship's bells.

Woodup Pool

   Green slime dangled from mooring ropes and a 'For Sale' sign was nailed to 'Emelia', a houseboat with plastic grass on the roof and seats for sun-bathing. The sun gleamed on the thick mud and yellowy green plants formed clumps on domes of higher land. The mud flats stretched

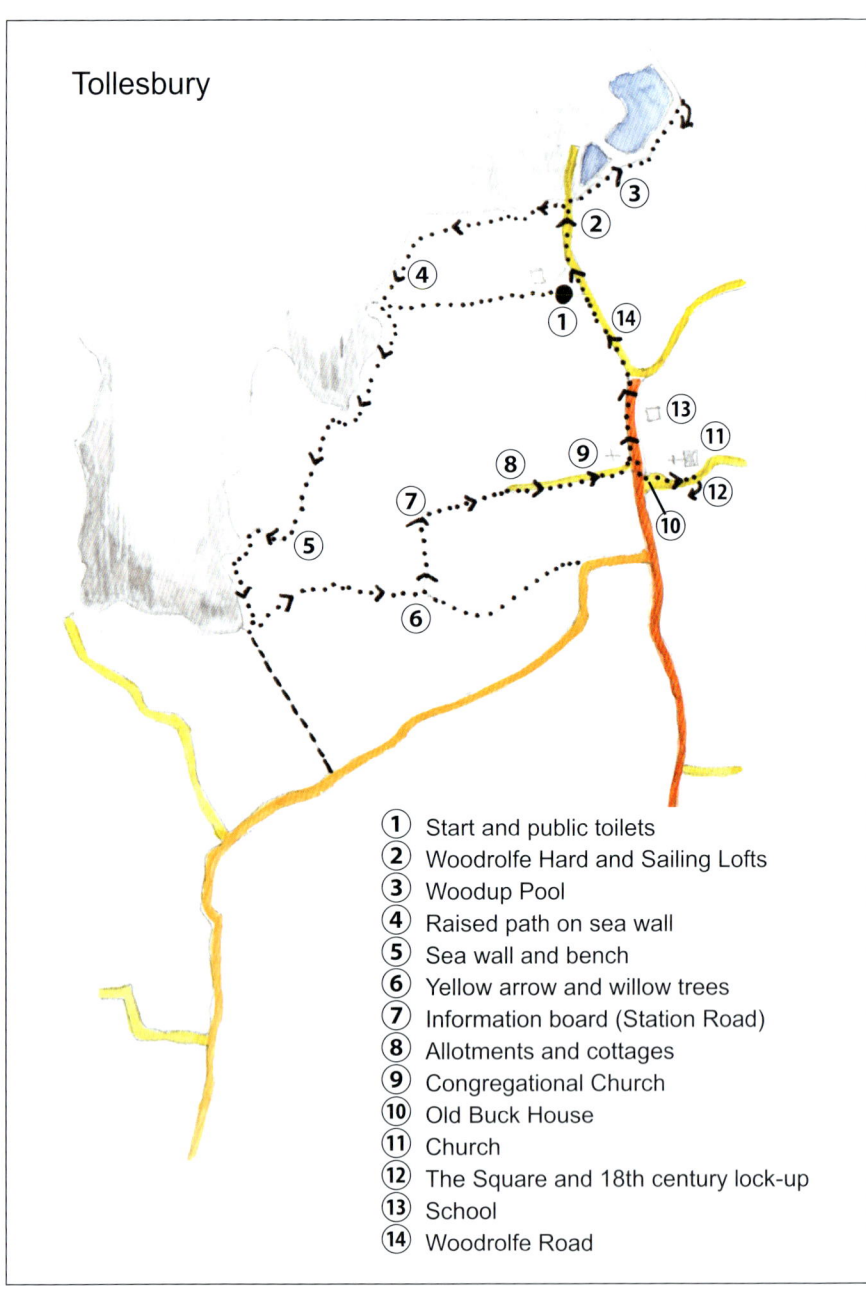

Tollesbury boats

away and away to Mersea Island. A black-headed gull swooped and perched on a random post.

The path on the raised bank allows far reaching views of either side. There is a paddock with horses and faraway rooftops inland and vast flatness with creeks and rivulets on your right.

In summer you can see bristly oxtongue with yellow daisy-like flowers and little white bumps on the leaves edging the path. Common sea lavender created a lilac haze of carpet on the salt marshes. Look too for wild carrot that forms tight little fists like bird's nests to protect its seeds. Listen for crickets and spot gatekeeper butterflies with brown circles on their wings or even little blue butterflies dancing among the yellow fleabane flowers.

You pass the sewage works soon (be prepared)! where the sea wall curls between land and sea.

There were skeletal forms of blackened trees standing knee-deep in rushes that whispered endlessly in the wind. And across the empty flatness a white egret perched on a lone post. Here there are steps down to the muddy creeks and brick defences shoring up the bank upon which I walked.

5. In a north-east direction you will see a red roofed cottage. The pathway curves and brings you to a wobbly bench just for two. Pause to sit awhile and soak in the stillness and sense of space, then drop down from sea wall towards track. (Across the field stands a white house and a bungalow nearby.)

Salt marshes

6. Turn left and left again along the lower edge of a field by a hedge-line, though there is no footpath sign.

   When I was here tractor tyres scored the path edged with a blackthorn hedge laden with berries.

   When you come to some silvery willow trees look for a yellow arrow which points right under the trees on your left as you walk along the side of field.

   The russet-brown of seeding dock accompanied the nettles in the verge and in the field germander speedwell shone like the bright blue stars.

   Turn left to dip through the hedge-line where brambles and yet more nettles flourish. Then walk through an overgrown patch before bearing left again.

7. Along a shady path edged with oak trees you come to an information board which tells you about Station Road. This was once a route for cattle from a nearby farm. At a concrete block turn right to walk back into Tollesbury but stop to enjoy the view of Mersea Island and the faraway wind turbines. Follow the stony track towards houses and parked cars.

8. Allotments soon appear on the right where , in summer, beans scramble up poles and dahlias splash vibrant colours beside the rhubarb. You pass a footpath sign pointing back down the track you have just crunched along. The cottages carry dates; 1884, 1885, 1907 and some bear names that link to the sea.

9. When you reach the Congregational Church where James Juniper is buried close to the door, alongside his aged wife, Elizabeth Susan, look for a welcome bench in the shade of a rowan tree. The church was built for dissidents in 1824. John Spurgeon was pastor here, the father of Charles Haddon Spurgeon - a famous preacher. This is the centre of Tollesbury. The 17th century King's Head sits on the corner of the Market Square. You can also see the tower of another church sporting a weather vane of a yacht.

10. Walk along the High Street to this church and pass Joe's cottage by Old Buck House, built in 1390, the oldest house in the village.

His granddaughter tells me that was the home of Joe Frost, who ran a butcher's in the nearby corner shop. He slaughtered animals in the yard at the back. He was ninety six when he died and the house has remained in the family ever since.

11. Turn left to find the church tower by the war memorial bearing soldier's names. The church here was built in 1090, originally an Anglo Saxon construction.

Tollesbury street

When I was there a sign told me that the church was open and I was welcome – the door was indeed open. Inside the flint tower bell ropes are looped above our heads. Look for the Seafarer's window depicting Peter and Jesus who is saying 'Follow Me and I will make you fishers of men'. A framed notice tells you about the boats featured here. The north window bears an ancient link with the sea. Can you find the fishing smack, coastal vessels and barges? Look too for an amusing message;

> 'You people here that pray, take care that in my church
> you do not sware as this man did.'

12. Outside in the Square (once called The Green) is another information board just by the 18th century village lock –up; for those who had 'over- imbibed' at one of the pubs. Go past Joe's Cottage again and turn right to pass a house bearing a painted name of the draper who once lived there. Walk down East Street passing Dove Cottage.

13. Look out for the School on your right.

14. Turn left down Woodrolfe Road which takes you back to the marina and industrial units. Along here is the car park and public toilets where our walk began.

Old boat, Tollesbury

Walk 14: West Hanningfield

This little village, north of Hanningfield Reservoir is only five miles from Chelmsford. Take a short drive at the end of the walk to see this huge stretch of water. It's well worth it.

Distance	3.2 miles or 5.2 km
Time	2 hours
Start	Pynnings Farm Lane. St Peter's Way
Terrain	Only gentle slopes – mainly very flat – stiles and kissing gates too
Map	OS Explorer 175 Southend on Sea & Basildon
Refreshments	The Three Compasses. 01245400447. Traditional pub with home-cooked food. Closed on Mondays. Café on Water. 01268712182 Open every day. 9am-4pm
Toilets	All the above
Getting there	From Chelmsford area take the B1007 towards Stock and watch out for The Ship and Ship Road on your left. Follow this road until you come to Holliday Hill and on a bend by Three Compasses Inn turn right into Lower Stock Road. Buses: Arrow Taxi runs from Chelmsford and First Essex 14 and 512 from Wickford to Chelmsford

1. Park in Pynnings Farm Lane outside some delightful properties. Here is St Peter's Way.

    Look out for timber-framed Gascoignes Farm. It was built between 1490 and 1540 but restored and altered in more recent years. The upper storey is jettied. Opposite is The Old Bakery – built in the 18th century with red-bricked chimney stacks. Beside a nearby house called Tarlings you will see a footpath sign by an iron gate and a kissing gate. This is where your journey begins as we join the forty-five mile long St Peter's Way for some of our route. Follow the path with the hedge-line on your right. The path gently climbs allowing pleasant views over fields to a farmstead.

Pynnings Lane, West Hanningfield.

I walked here in early autumn when old thistles and knapweed created a dry brown matting by the field edge where teasels grew tall. Pink clover was still in flower adding a touch of colour here and there and red rosehips gleamed in the hedgerow. As the path levelled out beneath oak trees, acorns crunched underfoot.

Hanningfield fields

2. At the field edge find a gap in the hedge and turn left to follow a yellow arrow, keeping the hedge – now of blackthorn – to your left. Across the fields is the Water Treatment Centre – the first hint of the reservoir.

3. The path begins to fall to a woodland ahead. There are more yellow arrows to reassure you of the route – bear right. Soon you find yourself skirting the trees where bracken grows as the path drops down to a kissing gate. Look out for a sign 'Danger. Deep Water'.

Here I took a diversion and followed a narrow path to find a wooden platform. I climbed the steps. This is Great Preston Lagoon Viewpoint. It was created in the 1950s. I stand and peer hopefully over channels of grey water and whispering reed beds. Will I see a marsh harrier? This is a Special Site of Scientific Interest (SSSI)– restored to seventeen hectares of reed beds in 2007. A sudden splash catches my attention as a big, brown fish jumps for flies before vanishing beneath the ripples. Just below me I can make out a small shoal of grey fish with pointed heads and orange tail fins. I must look them up when I get home. As I clamber down the steps an unseen coot calls as if bidding me goodbye.

Now in woodland bear right and follow the path as it ascends between hedges on either side that frame the fields beyond them. Look out for a bench made of planks by an oak tree and as another track crosses your path go straight on. (It may be muddy here after rain.) To your right are the pollarded trees of Blyth Hedges Wood – according to my map.

4. The path becomes surfaced and where a tall ash tree grows you come to the end of the wood. This is an old road – called Seaman's Lane. Now bracken, nettles and white cow mumble edge the footpath. Where thick ivy climbs an oak tree look out for the farm roof and white chimney stack of Steels Farm to your right.

5. Beyond a badger sett is a gate, a road with a red-bricked house on your right and a sign – Seaman's Lane, on your left. At Corner Cottage turn right into Leather Bottle Hill. Take care as there is no pavement and this road can be quite busy. Walk by The Glen – a thatched house on your left and The Willows painted white with a gravelled drive before the road dips.

6. Outside Steel's Farmhouse we say goodbye to St Peter's way as we turn right. Look for a stile and a narrow path that leads you between a hawthorn hedge and a wire fence to another stile that needs careful negotiation! Once safely over this you find yourself in open fields again.

7. March straight across the field towards the lovely countryside ahead and a marker oak tree.

At a ditch look for a yellow arrow and follow the field edge. At the lower corner bear left.

The muddy ground was scored with the patterns of tractor tyres and a jay screeched from the tall willow trees where the wind rustled the grey-green leaves.

At a white painted post turn right into the trees then left at another yellow arrow. Here the path narrows and creeps between overgrown brambles, tall nettles and sloe bushes. This is a place of scratches and stings! Soon you pass a pond on your left. When you come to a wooden footbridge bear

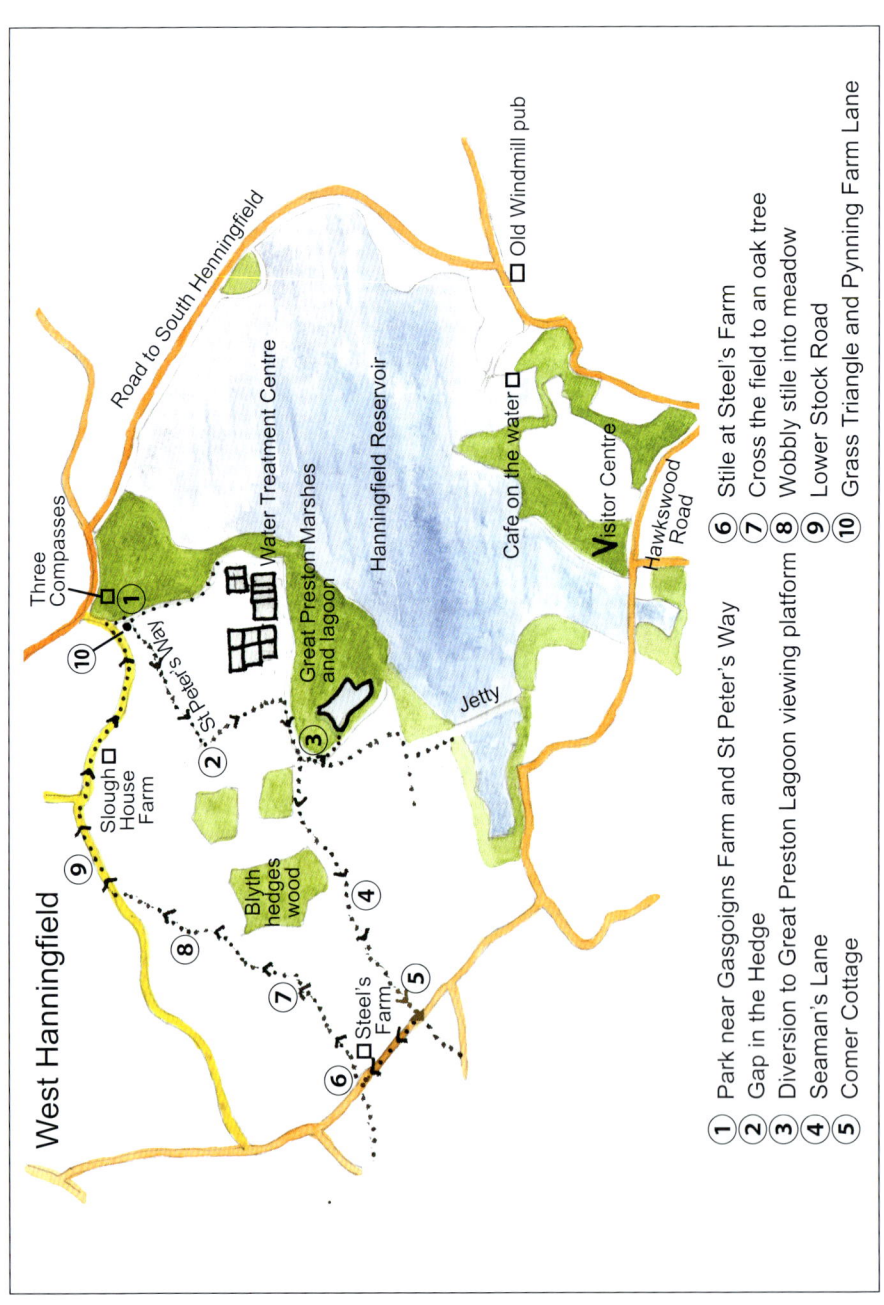

left. Keep the hedge on your left until you see another footbridge over a ditch. A yellow arrow confirms the way.

8. Look out for a white post on the left and a wobbly stile that takes you to an overgrown meadow.

This was a sheltered, sunny spot of long grass and thistles. To my left were beech trees and a mixed hedge of hazel, ash and field maple. Young pheasants scurried for cover as I approached.

Walk to another stile and footbridge over a dry ditch.

9. Here is Lower Stock road again. Turn right where streams flow on either side and pass Uplands bungalow, then Brooklands where you are warned to 'Beware of the Dogs'. Then comes Tristans with a red post box and Brick House Farm on the left. You soon see Slough House Farm with gabled wings, built in the seventeenth century.

West Hanningford lane

Behind the picket fence of Cob Cottage pale pink anemones grew tall and on the roof was a traction-engine weather vane. I heard the sound of a lawn mower – someone was cutting grass at the gabled Slough House Farm.

10. Walk on until you come to a triangle of grass in the road where pink roses climb a rowan tree and here is Pynnings Farm Lane and the place where you began.

I drove past The Three Compasses which serves good home-cooked food from 12-2pm. It was built in 1425 and has been a pub since at least 1758. Inside is a list of landlords from that long-ago date including Rosie who's been there for the last 49 years and intends to keep going! This could be a good place to stop but instead I turned right towards South Hanningfield. I wanted to find the reservoir. I turned left to pass the village sign and kept going until I saw the fenced bank of the reservoir on my right. I drove beneath pylons before I came to South Hanningfield Road where I turned right again. With the Old Windmill Pub on my left and a house called Cobblestones on my right I found a 'No Through Road' and a sign that welcomed me to Hanningfield Reservoir. I found a car park where greylag

Hanningfield Reservoir

geese waddled across a nearby picnic site. Here was my destination – The Café on the Water. On fine days there is decking outside where you can relax and simply gaze over the reservoir which was constructed in the hamlet of Peasdown in 1951.

Soon I was munching a sandwich and staring across the huge stretch of water which provides for 575,000 homes in Essex! The board says it holds 26 billion litres of water when full. Boats were drawn up below the little café where gulls squawked. I stopped to see a cormorant fly and watched a great crested grebe bobbing on the choppy surface.

There is a further walk from this café to Hanningfield Reservoir Visitor Centre and the 870 acres site. There are nature trails; bird hides; viewing platforms; toilets and refreshments. The Centre itself is the roost of soprano pipistrelle bats. Summer sees hundreds of swifts and swallows and on the water are gadwalls, pochards and tufted duck among the mallards and geese and below the surface are many fish – including trout. In the spring the woodlands are thick with bluebells.

Walk 15: Coggeshall

This walk is dedicated to my mum, Josie Martin, who has lived in Coggeshall for 89 years. Coggeshall is a lovely old town (some say village), with many timbered houses and a huge church St Peter ad Vincula - a legacy of the wool trade. Paycockes House owned by the National Trust is open to the public. The river Blackwater and The Abbey offer interesting walks, but I have chosen to explore the farmland on the eastern side of the noisy bypass, taking in the Marks Hall estate where once a fine mansion stood.

Distance	3.25 miles or 5.1 km
Time	2 hours but add on for a half way comfort stop
Start	Parking bay at the end of Tilkey Road or park behind the clock tower in the middle of the town but add 1½ miles to your walk
Terrain	Some gentle climbs, one or two steeper paths
Map	OS Explorer 195 Braintree & Saffron Walden
Refreshments	Marks Hall Visitor's Centre. 01376 563796. Serves breakfast from 10am Lunch until 2.30 and cakes until 3.45. Closes over Christmas and New Year. There are some lovely places to stop for a picnic including benches at The Owen Martin (my dad) Nature Reserve
Toilets	Marks Hall Visitor's Centre
Getting there	Take the A120 from Colchester to Braintree and exit the by-pass to take the B1024 into Coggeshall. Head for the centre of the village where the clock tower stands tall beside an old fashioned sweet shop. Drive up Stoneham Street passing Christ Church on your right and the former school on your left. Pass a left turning (Robinsbridge Road) and keep going straight until you see the 'No Through Road' sign. This is Tilkey Road – the name derives from Tile Kiln.

Getting there	There is a small area to park at the end of the road. Bus: First Essex number 70 from Colchester to Braintree twice an hour. Stops on Market Hill

Not far from the end of this road is a footpath leading to the Owen Martin Nature Reserve. Here are four acres of woodland and a big, deep pond. It is named after my father who gave so much to Coggeshall using his little grey tractor and trailer to do odd jobs around the village. As a boy he walked this way to school, never realising that one day a sign would bear his name. Dad left school aged fourteen. The headmaster told him he'd always be a clodhopper and indeed he did work on the land that he loved. Dad drove one of the first tractors ever used in Coggeshall – much to the envy of the other lads! Dad died in 2016. The local community decided to dedicate this Nature Reserve to him. Many say that he is still greatly missed. Do visit the site if you can.

Dad

1. Leave your car in a small parking bay and take the footpath by a gate, into rough overgrown woodland and scrubland where brambles, nettles and thistles edge your route and you need to duck beneath overhanging branches of blackthorn bushes. An open field appears on your right. There is a growing sound of traffic and soon you come to a concrete underpass adorned with scribbles of graffiti where lorries thunder over your head. Not the best start to any walk, but it is worth it, I promise.

    Yet somewhere nearby a blackbird sang – in brave defiance to the roar of the cars.

2. The well-trodden path goes on through a woodland tunnel of trees and crossing a tiny trickling stream until it reaches a fence. You will return to this spot later. Turn left to walk down towards Robin's Brook, keeping the fence to your right.

    Here is Cradle House now elaborately restored – but long ago the home of my father when he was a child. The weather boarded barn still stands –

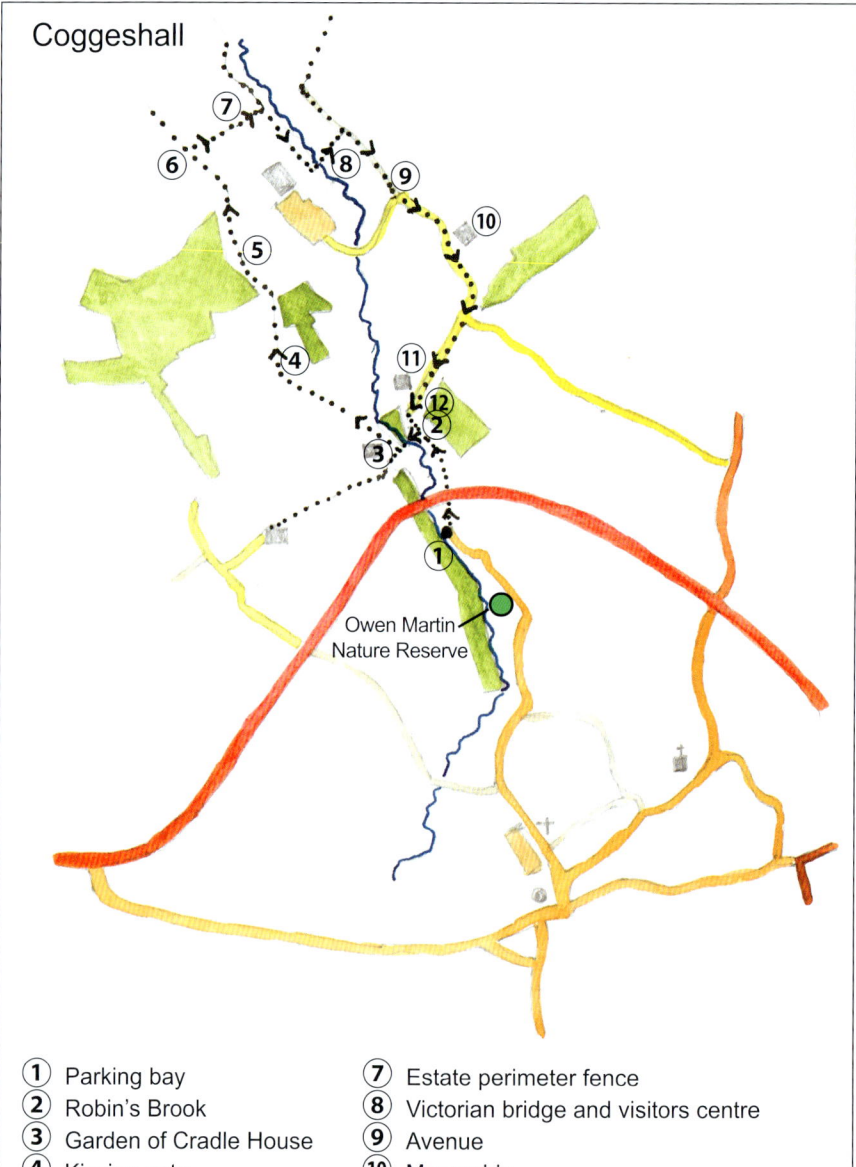

Coggeshall

1. Parking bay
2. Robin's Brook
3. Garden of Cradle House
4. Kissing gate
5. By Bungate Wood
6. Marks Hall Trail
7. Estate perimeter fence
8. Victorian bridge and visitors centre
9. Avenue
10. Marygolds
11. The Old Rectory
12. Yellow arrow to rejoin beginning of route

where three Suffolk punches, Duke, Daisy and Duchess were kept, when horses ploughed the land. The outside privy has long gone – as has the wash house and now the garden is flowers and neat lawns, but the thick chimney stack is still there.

3. At the footbridge over Robin's Brook, turn right to follow the yellow arrow on the bridge. Go by a wall, then across the garden and beside the tennis court to reach a fence and a metal kissing gate.

There are strange stories of Robin the woodcutter. It is said that you can hear his axe on a still winter's night.

4. Tramp across the paddock. The garden of the Old Rectory is on your right. When you come to some cherry trees take the grassy slope to find a narrow path between hedges, where in late spring wild roses bloom. Take care - nettles! Another metal kissing gate bearing a yellow arrow leads into a field.

All around me stretched a green sea of tall beans, but a trodden path cut a line straight across the vast field. As I climbed gently I saw the landmine crater in the adjacent field to my left, where today a willow tree has taken

Gatehouse Farm

root. And beyond it, Gatehouse Farm peeped over the hedges, its barn roof to my far left. This was my home as a young child. Then, my father was foreman at the farm and we lived in the tied house with its five bedrooms, two staircases, thick walls and mice! The outside privy and pump at the kitchen sink shaped very different childhood memories.

Go straight across the field following the path until you reach the corner of a wood. Your walk goes beside the wood across rough meadow land then straight across the next field. Ahead is Bungate Wood. Look for an arrow on a post half hidden by undergrowth. Far away to your right is a grand old house – Marygolds.

Marygolds

When I walked here, ripening wheat surrounded me. The wind created a crisp rustling sound and high above the wood a buzzard circled.

5. You come to another woodland on your right and another yellow arrow that points to a wooden footbridge. Pylons come into view. Bungate Wood is on your left with gnarled oak trees and a murky, green pond. There are lovely views of rolling countryside on your right with Marygolds still visible.

Little brown gatekeeper butterflies danced in the seeding grasses and from the wood came the gentle coo of a wood pigeon. The brambles bore pink flowers – promise of blackberries to come and a kestrel hovered by the field edge.

6. You will find yourself on a stretch of grass beside a low barbed wire fence. Beyond it is a wild flower meadow on your right. When you reach some newly planted saplings and a concrete road turn right. The field in front of you once was full of Nissen huts, for an American Airbase was here and the concrete road gives away this secret. Now you walk downhill with tall trees on your right and a sign tells you that you are on the Marks Hall Trail.

Coggeshall fields

7. Ahead are the grounds of the estate itself. At the T-junction turn right towards the Visitor Centre. A high fence edges the parkland with ornamental lakes, walled garden and sweeping lawns. A sign points you to the Iron Bridge.

Ox-eye daisies, yellow bird's foot trefoil and purple knapweed clumped together around willow trees beside the gravelled path. The Visitor's Centre appeared ahead and a kiosk for tickets into the lovely grounds of Marks Hall where one ancient oak tree survives. The estate is open Tuesday - Sunday from April until October and at weekends during winter months. I get a permission sticker to allow me into the café and spotless toilets. Hot chocolate and ginger-treacle cake soon recharge my energy. Outside by a walnut tree are picnic tables for sunny days. Sandwiches with salad garnish or jacket potatoes are available if you're hungry.

I remember Marks Hall estate when it was derelict and abandoned. The hall itself had long gone but the brick-edged lakes were overgrown and barely accessible. When they cleared them many rusty old bicycles were recovered – 'borrowed' from the village by soldiers wanting to get home.

8. Go over the Victorian iron bridge pausing to see water lilies and dragonflies in summer. Then follow the steep track passing picnic benches on a grassy slope. Old iron railings line the gravelly path and more brambles grow on your left.

9. At the top is a tarmacked road where a sign points left or right, we turn right to walk down an avenue of horse chestnut trees with wild meadow land falling away on our right. There are signs to tell us about Marks Hall. We follow the 'Way Out' sign through white painted wooden gates.

10. Here is Marygolds behind a high wooden fence. From the arching in the windows are wonderful views across the fields and woods where we have just walked. The road drops, there is no pavement so take care. In the valley is Robin's Brook again, then the road climbs steeply towards a signpost.

11. Turn right at the fork towards the Old Rectory. Again you can see the barns of Gatehouse Farm across the fields of wild flowers. The white railings soon appear – the entrance to the house with its honey coloured bricks and slate roof. A thick laurel hedge provides privacy from curious passers-by.

I remember a kindly lady, Mrs. Leftley who lived here with her daughter, Helen who had been dropped down the stairs when she was a baby, the story goes – by a maid. Helen was left with severe brain-damage as a result.

12. At the gate a yellow arrow sign takes us to the route we trod before.

A scattering of pine cones littered the way and sunlight dappled the path. Once, before the by-pass came, this was a quiet, well-kept meadow where animals grazed. The woodland was a place of beauty full of bluebells in May – the place for picnics and games of hide and seek.

Retrace your steps bearing left to cross the little stream and pass the tangled hedges, tall nettles and thistles – with noise of traffic offending your ears as the underpass appears ahead. Keep going until you reach the houses of the village and, if you started here, your car.

Coggeshall street

Walk 16: Great and Little Maplestead

This is a circular walk, up and down dale, in beautiful North Essex countryside. It follows field edges mainly, so sturdy shoes are needed. It starts and ends in Great Maplestead but visits the little round church at Little Maplestead too.

Distance	3½ miles or 5.5 km
Time	2 hours or more
Start	Car park by playing field opposite Great Maplestead School
Terrain	Some steep hillsides
Map	OS Explorer 195 Braintree & Saffron Walden
Refreshments	I would recommend taking a picnic. There is a bench in the churchyard looking over the lovely views in the undulating landscape as well as a toilet in the church porch. (Hopefully unlocked)! Or sit on the hill top for stunning views that dismiss the saying; 'Essex is flat!' Castle Hedingham Village shop – a few minutes drive – sells sandwiches and cakes. In Halstead is The Little Book Café. www.littlebookcafe.co.uk 01787 475647 – booking needed
Toilets	At St Giles Church porch
Getting there	The Maplesteads are three miles north of Halstead and seven miles from Sudbury. It is a thirty minute drive from Colchester. No regular bus service. No train. The A 131 from Halstead to Sudbury or the A1017 both go by the turnings to these villages

1. Start in the centre of Great Maplestead. There is free parking by the village hall or spaces by the playing field. From here just a little way down the hill take some steps up the bank on the opposite side of the road. These will take you beside the churchyard where immediately you see gently rolling hills to your left as the land falls away beneath you. The path leads

Maplestead fields

you into the church yard of St Giles – the ancient church which squats low amid trees, guarding the village from its hilltop position.

If you have time, wander down the path to the gate to find the headstone of John Scott Martin (on your left). He was the chief Dalek in the 'Doctor Who' television series. As well as being a church warden here, he lived in a stone cottage opposite the church gate. The church too is worth a peep inside. It is over 700 years old, with a 12th century apse and is full of shadows. There are some interesting memorials and the embroidered kneelers were hand made by local people.

2. Look for a yellow arrow at the left hand corner of the churchyard and walk diagonally across the grass to find yourself on the edge of a field that drops down into the valley where a stream flows.

When I walked here it was very muddy and my boots became heavier with each step. I made a beeline for the oak tree ahead. I paused to turn back to see the church. A buzzard circled overhead, his great wings stretched wide.

3. Look for another footpath sign and walk by a ditch towards tall willow trees. Here you will find a path that leads to a gap in the hedge where a footbridge crosses the little brook. Now the route begins to climb very steeply and soon more lovely views appear all around you, indeed this is one of the loveliest walks in this patch of North Essex. You will pass two oak trees – one appears to be standing on tiptoes – some roots growing vertically.

   The chugging sound of a tiny tractor is carried on the wind from a faraway field and to my right an isolated pink thatched cottage is tucked into the hillside below.

4. You come to a gateway on the other side of the field and now the path drops to the little road which you cross to find Mill Lane. On the left are semi-detached houses. There are deep banks either side as the road falls to an old weather-boarded barn before it rounds a corner.

5. Climb over a stile by iron gates on your left near to Mill Farm and follow a footpath bearing left to a gap in the hedge, where in summer bracken grows. (Don't walk up the slope as I did, but keep to the left.)

   Mill Farm nestles in the quiet valley of undulating fields. A horse in a paddock lifts his head to watch me for a moment, then resumes his grazing.

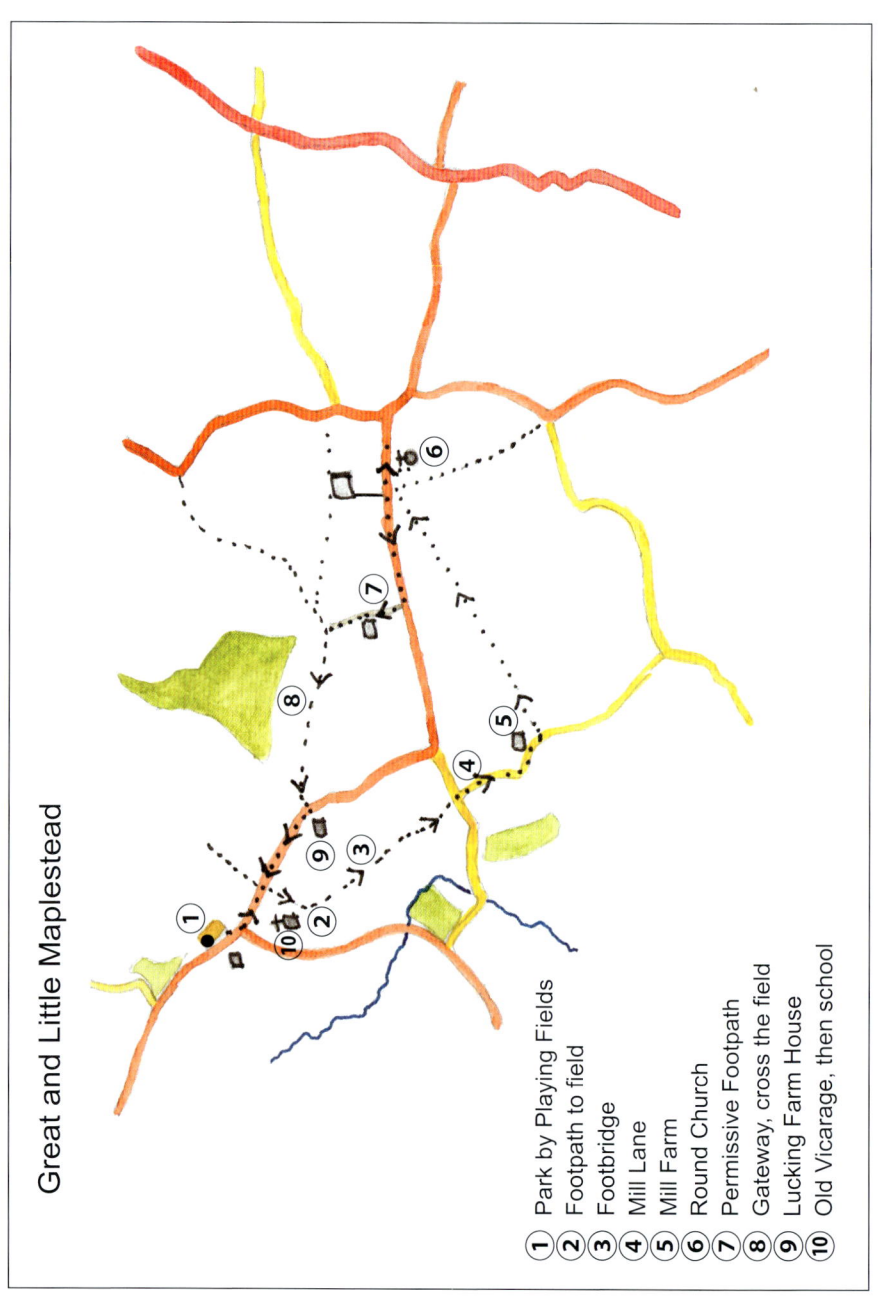

Maplestead landscape

Follow the path some distance along the field edge with the tall hedgerow to your right. In autumn it is abundant with berries and in spring adorned with wild roses. You will eventually reach some red-brick farm cottages and the road.

St John the Baptist, Maplestead

6. Turn right – for a detour to visit the tiny church of St John the Baptist. It was built of flint in 1335 and is one of only five round churches in England. If the door is unlocked, go inside to find an ancient stone font (1080) where babies were fully immersed! Near the altar are small wooden pews.

The church and the Manor house opposite were bequeathed to the Knights of St John in Jerusalem (The Knights Hospitallers) in 1836 when the order was re-established. They ran a hospital in Little Maplestead and because of their good work in the community, Henry VIII did not close them down during the reformation. In the church is a table full of information about this ancient order if you wish to learn more. Today we know them for their first aid, ambulances and an eye hospital in Jerusalem.

7. Crunch back down the gravelly drive and turn left to walk a short distance down the country road. You will see the drive to Little Lodge Farm. It is a bridleway with a permissive footpath. It takes you beyond the house to a left hand turning by an old gatepost adorned with ivy. Walk by the electric fence beside a paddock with the farmhouse to your left. It has a huge central chimney stack. Look for another footpath sign that points you to a marker post and soon you will see the rooftops of the village again.

8. The next gate leads into a field where the path crosses centrally.

   This field had been recently ploughed and the footpath was not clear. I tramped across yet more mud. Heavy boots again! The 'Beware of the Bull' sign did not deter me but thankfully the field was empty!

   Cross the stream and head diagonally towards the farm buildings, cottages and the road.

   In *the barn where several tractors stood a heap of muck steamed gently, giving out an old-fashioned country smell.*

Maplestead

9. At another gateway turn right onto the road which leads up and back to the village. Behind an arched wooden door in a wall is Lucking Farm House with its three storeys. Eight metres west of the house is a red brick oast house. It was built around 1700. In the 19th century there was a hop yard in the farmyard and it was still in use until 1870. There are several pretty cottages along here. Look out for Mossings, The Forge and a plaque on the wall at The Smithy. Bernard Stevens, a composer lived and worked here from 1916 to 1983. In 1946 he won a prestigious prize for a piece of music called *The Victory Symphony*. The work that celebrated the end of the war, was premiered at the Royal Albert Hall.

10. As you approach the village you will see the tall chimneys of the Old Vicarage rising above the trees on your left.

   Local people remember the Reverend Belben shooting pigeons from an attic window! He was quite a character; indeed one of his phrases was 'as happy as a mosquito in a nudist camp!'

   You will pass the School sign as well as the village hall on your right. There are also some newly built houses of imaginative design. The village is growing, despite the fact that there is no longer a shop or a public house. Pause to see the Victorian school which was built by Mrs Mary Gee using her own money in 1863. Later it was given to the parish and the vicar and churchwardens became trustees. Then it was named St Giles School.

   Drive two miles to Castle Hedingham for village shop (sandwiches). Or go to nearby Halstead where there are several cafés. One of my favourites is The Little Book Café but you will need to book as it's very popular. The walls are lined with books for browsing and they serve amazing Welsh Rarebit!

Walk 17: Wrabness

Wrabness sits on the banks of the River Stour estuary not far from Harwich and the coast. This walk enjoys views across the water and saltmarshes as well as dipping inland to explore narrow lanes. Check the tides though before you set off, at high tide the coastal path disappears under water for an hour or two, in some places.

Distance	3.6 miles or 5.8 km
Time	2 hours
Start	Station car park (small fee) or roadside in the village
Terrain	Fairly level, bar an extended uphill stretch to the church
Map	OS Explorer 184 Colchester, Harwich & Clacton
Refreshments	The Community Shop. Open 9am-1pm and 3-6pm. Harwich has many eateries if you need something more substantial
Toilets	The Community Shop
Getting there	Take the A120 to Harwich. Beyond Wix look for a left hand turn to Wrabness with its station. This is Primrose Lane. There are no buses but CrossCountry Trains run an hourly service to and from Colchester every day

1. A good place to start is at the community shop, on a bend of the road near the station. Here you can buy drinks, cakes or ice-creams, both before and after your walk. There is water for the dog and paintings by local artists, if you want a keepsake and there is a toilet.

   In Black Boy Lane (named after the pub that was) turn into the No Through Road to pass Seagull Cottages and go over the railway bridge.

2. The road becomes a gravel track. 'Woodlands' stands on your right, before you come to other cottages with pretty gardens. (In summer honeysuckle here gives out sweet fragrance) Then comes a stable yard.

Wrabness to docks

> *Edging the path were ferns, ox-eye daisies and purple mallow flowers as the path entered countryside. A lovely view appeared to the right where the faraway cranes of Felixstowe docks graced the skyline. Horses grazed in the paddock and on my left a strange holiday let has been built.*

The path drops between tall nettles beside a field (left). Here you glimpse the water ahead. There is a shadowy woodland to your right called East Grove.

> *Dog-roses scramble along a fence and swallows skim the wheat in summer.*

3. Bear left at the end of the field with the mud flats and river now on your right beyond a line of oak trees. The narrow path tracks the river bank – or sea wall perhaps? Soon there is a deep ditch to your left and stubby trees where the creek winds through the salt marshes.

4. Look out for Shore Farm on your left, built of red brick with an impressive porch and horses in the paddock. Can you spot the cannon? You come to a flood gate and here you drop down by a murky pond to walk along the lower edge of the next field. The track is wider here.

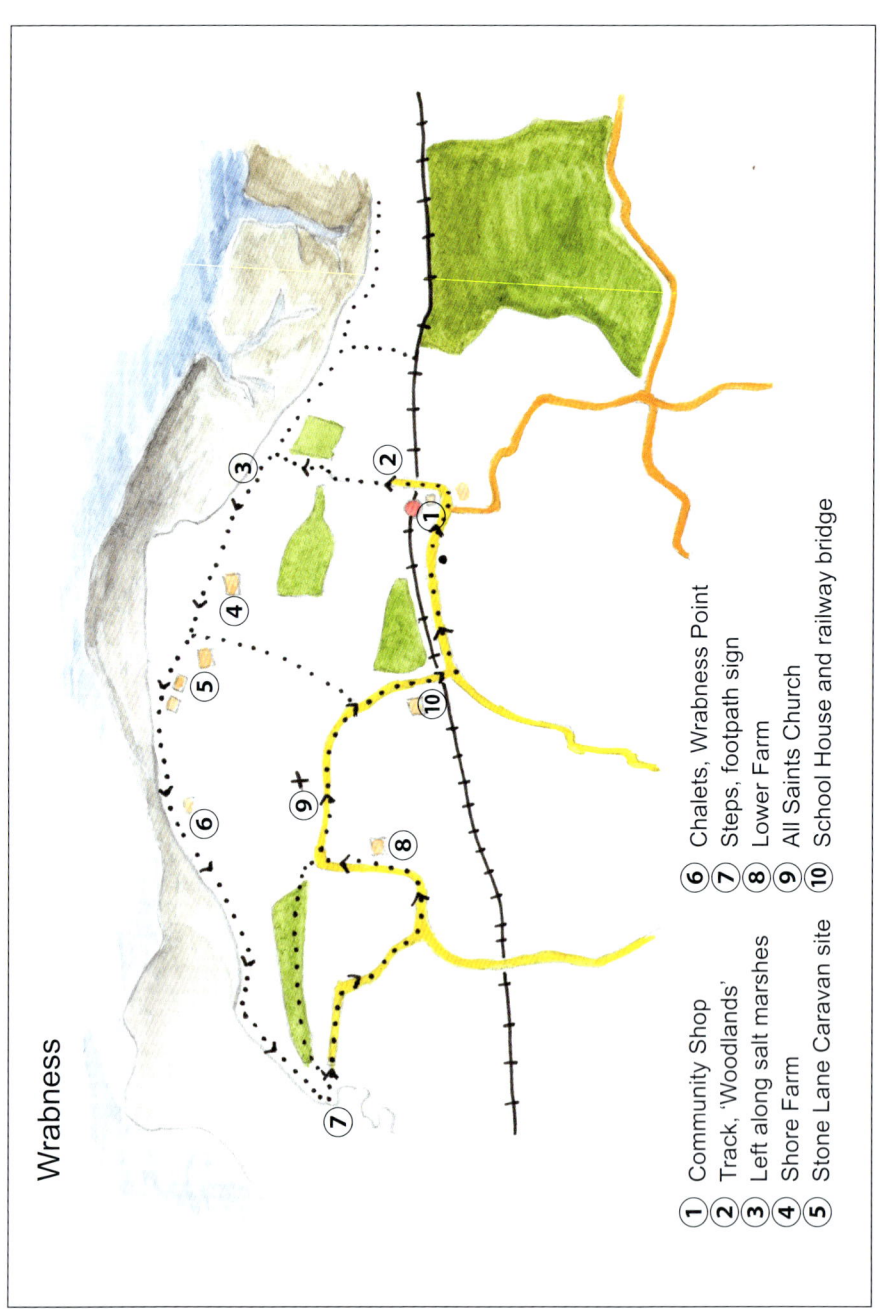

Clumps of bindweed and mayweed flourished here alongside red poppies that added bright dots of crimson.

5. You reach Stone Lane Caravan Site. Look for a yellow arrow that takes you right, then left over the bank to walk across the salt marsh, crossing a footbridge to the shore. This is Balhaven Salt Marsh a Site of Special Scientific Interest (SSSI) and a sign tells us not to pick the flowers!

   I found sea purslane and lesser sea spurrey as well as scurvy grass, once eaten by sailors I am told. There was the smell of salt from drying weed and the crunch of shingle under my boots; a dead crab, its white under-belly gleaming in the sun and the gentle sound of lapping water. Upturned boats warm in the sun and black shells on the smooth sand created a sea-side feel to this stretch of the walk.

6. Walk by a haphazard collection of padlocked chalets to your right as you follow the estuary that curves to the left at Wrabness Point. On the far bank of the estuary you will see a grand building. This is the Royal Hospital School purpose-built on its 200 acre site in 1933. The school was founded in 1712 for boys from seafaring families. Once it was housed in Greenwich in the building which today is the National Maritime Museum. Now it is co-educational, for boarders and day students who all learn to sail!

   Be warned; this path becomes impassable at high tide. So check before you set out.

Wrabness shoreline

The chalets were weekend hideaways I presumed, as there was nobody about as I came this way. Plastic chairs were stacked on decking built high to be out of reach of the tide. Little boats were moored or slowly moving on the wide river. There was a lovely sense of open space here. Shelduck preened by the pools at the mud flats and across the water was the old London Road, written about by Daniel Defoe. Linger here before you go inland and if you're blessed, as I was, you'll hear a cuckoo calling.

7. When you come to a footpath sign, take the steps down towards a metal gate. Ignore another sign that points you through trees, instead follow the road as it climbs to Wall Lane and levels out between high hedges that cast dappled shadows on sunny days.

Everything was quiet bar a chaffinch singing nearby, then came the sound of a train somewhere to my right. I'd forgotten the railway was so near.

Wrabness cottage

8. At a triangle of grass central in the road where buttercups glow golden in summer turn left to walk up hill for some distance. You pass a spot for Green Woodland Burials before you come to Lower Farmhouse with a barn conversion. Now it gets steep (leg-aching time)! Outside Number 7, a pretty cottage up a brick path, pause to look back for the view is good; farm buildings, roof-tops and faraway cottages dotted among thick woodland and fields. Ignore a footpath on your left.

9. Now you are in Church Road and no surprise, here is the Norman flint church of All Saints with its wooden bell cage for there is no spire or tower. The churchyard is a haven for wild things – waist high in ox-eye daisies in summer. Go inside if the door is unlocked.

A sign in the porch read 'O God make the doorway of this church wide enough to receive all who need human love...' I stepped inside into the stone coolness where the sun shone pale through unadorned windows. Hymn number 310 and 499 announced themselves on the board on the wall. Outside sparrows chirped noisily – interrupting the quietness around me. I learned that the doorways are Norman and the 17th century bell cage is

Wrabness farm

listed; a 13th century coffin lid was found under the floor and now is in the south porch. I also read that a bell is rung to 'summon us to divine service'.

Outside at the gate you turn left to walk further along the road. There is another farm on your left. Look for a bench and views of the Stour estuary. There is an information board too.

Bell cage

10. Now you come to more houses as you are approaching Wrabness once again. Pass Maypole House on your right and The Old School House – a clue to the past. Then you find yourself on the railway bridge. Turn left to walk the pavement back into the village. Semi-detached houses line the road on the right while the railway runs adjacent on the left.

I stopped to buy green pepper plants at a cottage gate, poking my money in the letter box of the front door.

Soon you will come to the community shop again. There is a little garden area as well.

I drove the few miles into Harwich in search of the Ha'Penny Pier where I'd been told you can buy snacks. Here I sat at a picnic table with a sandwich and cool drink enjoying the sights and sounds of the harbour. A fishing boat, 'Our Bess' bobbed on the grey, rippling water, orange buoys tied to its sides and green weed dangling from its mooring ropes. Black headed gulls wheeled and circled above and people sat licking ice-creams that dribbled in the hot sun. A flag fluttered where the harbour ferry was docking, manned by sunburned men in yellow T-shirts. A lovely end to my walk at Wrabness.

Walk 18: Little Easton

Two miles north west of Dunmow in the Chelmer Vale is Little Easton with its 16th century manor house overlooking the church and The Forgotten Gardens of Easton Lodge.

Distance	3¾ miles or 6.1 km
Time	2 hours or more at a gentle pace
Start	Duck Street in the village centre near the War Memorial
Terrain	Steep in places
Map	OS Explorer 195 Braintree & Saffron Walden
Refreshments	The Stag in Duck Street. 01371870214 Thursday to Sunday. Pre-booking needed. Take- aways available
Toilets	In the pub
Getting there	Leave the A120 at Great Dunmow and take the B184 to Thaxted. Look for a left turning to Little Easton about one mile out of the town. There is no regular bus service

1. Park the car somewhere in the centre of the village. The Stag has a car park.

   I parked in Butcher's Pasture just off the main road near the village sign and war memorial.

2. & 3. Walk past The Stag public house and the Old Stag Cottage (former public house) with its long low thatched roof and wander down the hill passing Hill Cottage on your right.

Little Easton sign

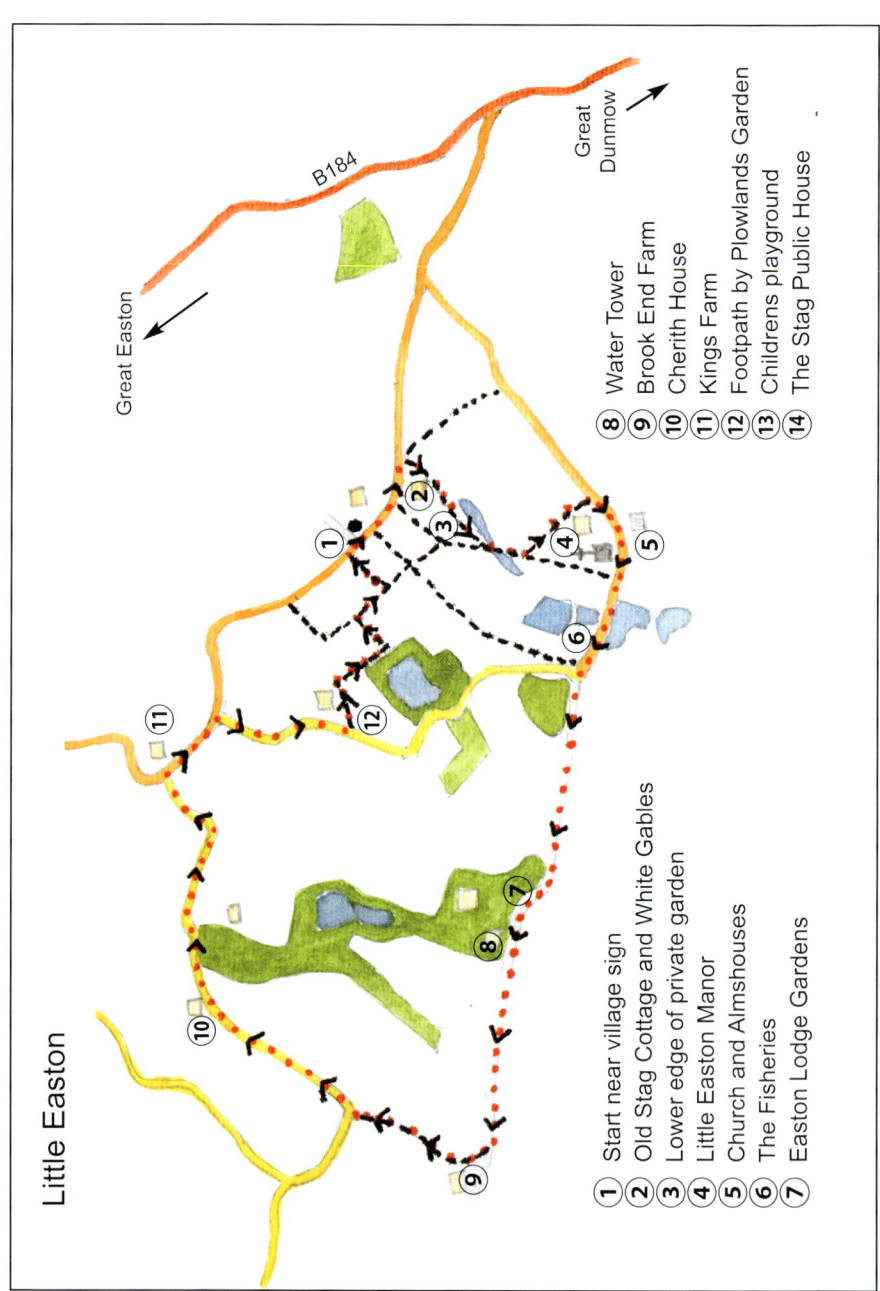

When you reach White Gables find a narrow footpath between high fences where ivy scrambles. It leads to rough wasteland (a haven for rabbits) on your left and a paddock to your right. There are tall poplars and graceful willow trees.

4. At a kissing gate you enter someone's garden where in spring, daffodils flower. There are ponds and a stream on your left. As you leave, the path travels uphill with open fields on either side where one old oak tree stands a lonely sentinel.

5. The path curves and ahead are the pink walls of The Manor with barns and theatre. Look for a yellow arrow that points you into the churchyard over a stile.

You get a better view of the 17th century Manor if you peep over the churchyard wall. The tithe barn was converted to a theatre in 1913 and you can still see shows there. The Manor serves as a wedding venue today. There are extensive grounds and the ponds are stocked with mirror carp and tench.

Little Easton Manor

Across the road you will see the alms-houses built by Lord Maynard for four poor widows. Take time to explore Little Easton church – built in the 12th century.

Little Easton almshouses

I found a door in the tower and stood gazing down a long central aisle – perfect for a bride on her wedding day. The church clock ticked – a deep, regular sound above my head. A sign read; 'Leave it not without one prayer to God for yourself and for those who minister here'.

On the wall was a roll of rectors – the first Robert Hereward served here in 1336. There is a mausoleum to the Maynards in a chapel adjoining the chancel where carved figures cradle skulls and Lady Fisher lies beneath the flagstones. I pause beneath two 1990 windows commemorating the link with the American Airforce (Easton Lodge).

Can you find the old stocks in the churchyard?

6. Walk through the gate and head down the road where wooden gateposts stand near Church Lodge (17th century) on your right. You soon come to The Fisheries, huge well-stocked ponds set behind iron railings on either side of the road where anglers can buy a day ticket for £15.

Canada geese paddled towards me – hopefully eyeing me for bread and glossy mallards stood motionless on the muddy bank, their heads tucked beneath their wings.

7. The road rises steeply. Ignore a closed sign – as this applies to the Forgotten Gardens of Easton Lodge. This windswept stretch of the walk has wide open fields on both sides. Soon you reach the gardens themselves where rooks caw in tall trees and mistletoe dangles.

The gardens are open on occasional days during the summer months, from 11.30am to 5pm. In February there are Snowdrop Sundays. There is a small entrance fee but children are free. Check **www.easton lodge.co.uk** *for* *further information or phone 01371 876979. An imposing Elizabethan manor house once stood here surrounded by landscaped gardens. There was a temple, a brick dovecote; an icehouse and three avenues of trees. In 1847 a fire destroyed most of the mansion but it was rebuilt in Victorian Gothic style. Daisy Maynard inherited it – at the age of three – much to the disgust of the wider family. They threw butter at the portrait of Daisy's grandfather!*

Daisy turned down marriage to Queen Victoria's youngest son marrying instead the Earl of Warwick. She continued to develop the gardens. Grand parties were held here, with guests including A.A. Milne, George Bernard Shaw and Charlie Chaplin. In 1918 another fire (started by a pet monkey) destroyed the house. During 1939 the estate was requisitioned by the War Office. As the years went by everywhere became overgrown with brambles and tall nettles until in 1971 the Creaseys bought some of the estate and began many years of restoration. By 2014 much of the garden had been reclaimed.

Low aeroplanes remind you that Stansted Airport is only a few miles away. Another sign says 'Strictly Private' but my map shows clearly that a public footpath passes along here.

8. Further along you come to Warwick House behind sturdy iron gates and Stableyard Cottages and a large brick water tower built in 1902.

   On the left you will soon see rounded Nissen huts – work places today for small businesses.

9. When you reach Brook End Farm with its stable-yard, look for a yellow arrow, for here we leave the road.

   Horses heads peered over green stable doors as a booted girl wearing plastic gloves wheeled a barrow of straw. Harnesses and other tack hung on nails and I heard the splash of water – as another girl sprayed a white horse with a hose, grooming him to perfection.

   The footpath creeps between paddocks to reach a copse and a muddy stream. Another arrow (bridleway) points right where the path drops down to the stream.

   This patch can be wet after heavy rain.

10. You soon come to a road which rises between high, grassy banks to Broxted Hill. Now you can enjoy far-reaching views of rolling fields and houses in the valley. The road curves and falls again. Cherith House stands behind an impenetrably thick hedge. The sewage works appear on your left – there is a hum of more than machinery! Scots pine edge the woodland to your right. Look for the gate pillars of Perryfields before the road begins to climb, quite steeply. You can see the rooftops of Great Easton to your left.

In the grass verge pale yellow primroses and purple violets added colour. The brown fields dropped down to a stream. The wind was chill.

11. At the T-junction turn right to Little Easton. You will see Kings Farm. This is a busier road but we only walk along it for a short stretch, nevertheless watch out for traffic. Take a right turn into Laundry Lane where the road climbs steeply to Plow Lands on your left. Here is a chicken coop in a garden of apple trees. If you walk this way in springtime there is a sea of yellow daffodils.

12. As the garden ends look for a footpath signpost half hidden in the hedge on your left. This takes you along a field edge by a deep ditch. Turn right onto the next field and continue with the hedge on your right. The path

drops down to the stream. At the lower corner bear left where a yellow arrow points you over the stream.

13. Walk up the hill on a grassy pathway until you come to a children's play park then follow the arrow sign back to the village. You pass a cricket pavilion where heavy rollers wait for sunny days. The path becomes a stony track as you reach the back gardens of the houses.

There were neat stacks of logs by a barn conversion and pretty hanging baskets adding welcome colour against the white walls of Tithe Cottage.

This is Glebe Lane. It leads to the road and your starting place.

14. Now you turn right – back in the centre of the village. Soon you will see Butcher's Pasture and the War Memorial and a few more steps takes you to The Stag.

We perused the lunch-time menu and found the Golden Years pages offering reduced rates on weekdays. We chose vegetable lasagne with salad and chips – we declined the sticky toffee pudding! The dining room was cosy and comfortable. If the day had been sunny a large garden behind the pub offered an alternative. Sandwiches and jacket potatoes are also available and Sunday is roast dinner day.

Walk 19: Pleshey

When William the Conqueror claimed our lovely land in 1066 he rewarded one of his battle commanders Geoffrey de Mandeville with Pleshey and it was he who promptly built the motte and bailey castle with a deep moat which is still at the centre of this quiet little village, north west of Chelmsford.

Distance	Just under 4 miles or 6.5 km. A circular walk to explore the village, the earthworks and the surrounding countryside
Time	2+ hours
Start	At the Village Hall, near the church where the car park is free
Terrain	Gentle slopes but fairly level over all
Map	OS Explorer 183 Chelmsford & The Rodings
Refreshments	Leather Bottle serves only drinks and crisps. 01245 237291
Toilets	The pub
Getting there	The B1008 lies North East of Pleshey and the A1060 lies South West. Look for signposts. Buses run from Chelmsford four times a day.

1. Park at the Village Hall. Walk to nearby Holy Trinity church and hopefully it will be unlocked. There is a central tower. It is an attractive building – once part of the College of Canons which was shut down by Henry VIII in 1546.

   Sadly when I walked this way the church was firmly locked despite a note on the website which said, 'Open for prayer from dawn to dusk.' Hmm.

   Continue towards the main street of the village and you will come to the House of Retreat owned by the Anglican Chelmsford Diocesan. Here is a place for prayer.

A sign welcomes visitors to use the space for quiet reflection and I determine to visit the chapel at the end of my walk.

Opposite the entrance is the White Horse once a public house, bearing a clue to its past. Can you see it? As you walk along the pavement there are pretty cottages on either side.

Holy Trinity church

2. Look for a footpath sign (right) and a track to Pleshey Castle itself. There is a deep moat (fenced) with a bridge spanning it leading to padlocked gates. Beyond these is the mound, some 15 metres (30 foot) high, one of the biggest in England. Across the grass there are steps leading up to a beacon point. Telephone 01245 237291 to make an

The White Horse

appointment if you'd like to access it. In the 12th century it was fortified with a stone castle. In 1629, when it had become a ruin, the masonry was dismantled leaving just the motte and earthworks. But these are impressive enough!

I wish I'd made an appointment; it looks a wonderful place to explore. As I stood on the bridge a line of fluffy black and yellow ducklings trailed after their mother in the moat below where an unseen moorhen called. From the undergrowth came the sudden burst of a wren's song. I retraced my steps back to the road.

3. Turn right to walk along the street passing the Old Post House (once a Post Office and shop). Rose Cottage is thatched with twinkling lattice windows. Soon you will see Back Lane on the other side of the road.

In Spring there are cherry trees thick with blossom here.

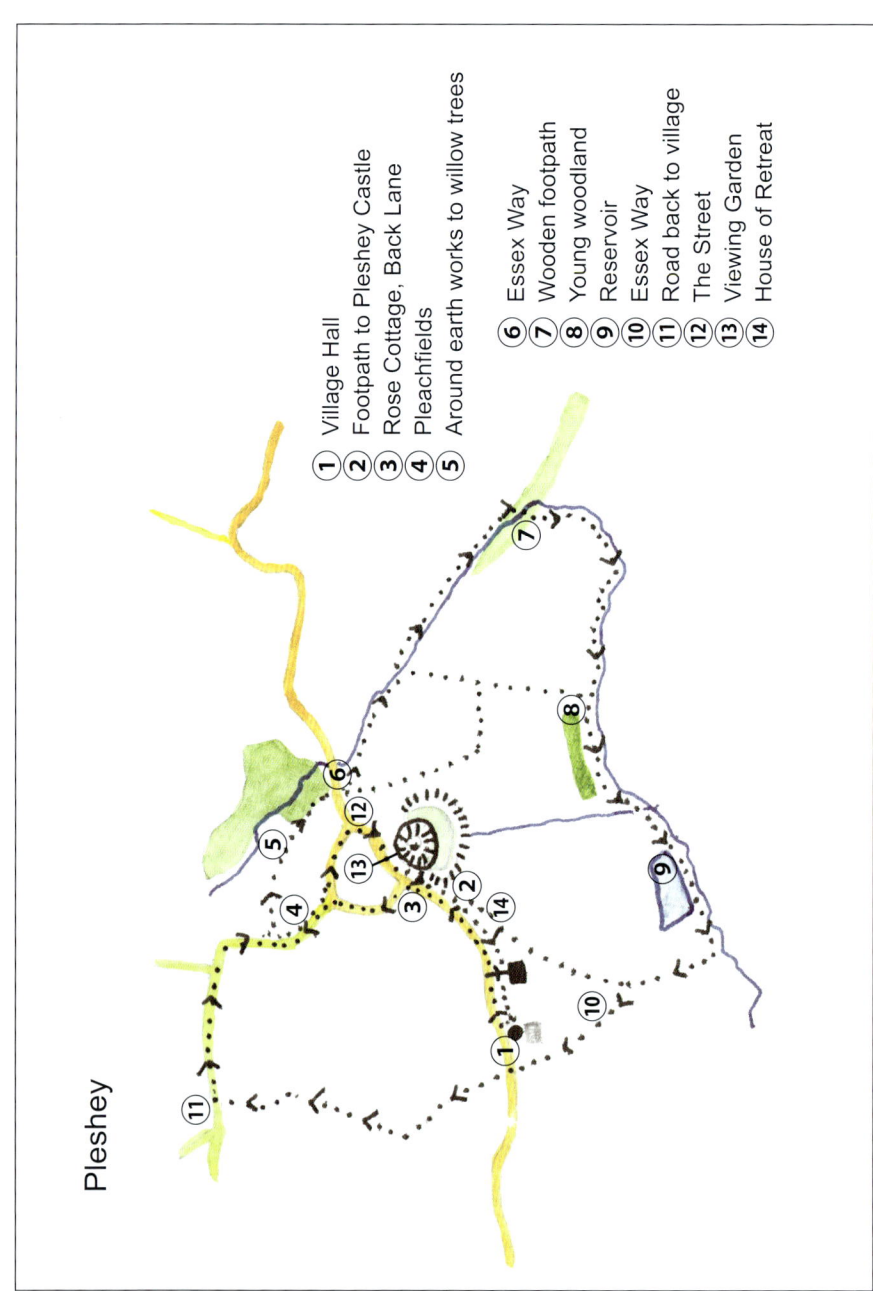

4. Turn into Back Lane by a pump with a memorial sign and ahead is a huge willow and more thatched cottages with magnolia trees in the colourful gardens. When you come to The Forge turn left to walk towards Pleshey Grange. There is a children's playground on the right if you have youngsters with you. Ahead you will see Pleachfields, a substantial red brick house opposite Pippins – a storybook cottage with a thick thatched roof.

Back Lane

Pleaching originated from an old French word – pleche meaning to intertwine or weave together. When the deep moat was dug the thorn hedges were planted on its banks and woven to create an impenetrable barrier to any hostile locals who resented their French overlords.

5. Now you are leaving the village. On your right is a footpath sign pointing around the curve of the earthworks. Now the field is on the left and the deep ditch, right. The houses are perched upon the steep bank, their garden boundary ending with earthworks. You will reach a willow plantation where the ground becomes damp and swampy. Bear right through the trees and here is the busy road.

6. Take care as you cross for the traffic is fast, to a footpath sign by the metal gate of a water pumping station (I think). It directs you along the Essex Way between a fence and ditch on a well-trodden, narrow path. (It isn't easy to spot.) A little further on water trickles from a pipe at the effluent point and another Essex Way sign can be seen. This confirms you are on track!

I walked along the lower field edge by a deep ditch where a tiny stream flowed. The landscape was opening up wide all around me. Partridges scurried for cover as I approached. There was nothing but space, fields and sky! In the verge by my feet, goose-grass, docks and cow mumble grew.

7. Keep following the ditch line straight along the footpath until you come to a wooden footbridge. Telegraph poles march across the field as the path

curves. Look for a footpath sign that directs you down steep steps on your right, through a hedge-line and into a thicket. Here is another wooden bridge then more steps. Now turn left to walk along the field edge with trees to your left. Once you have left the woodland behind look for the distant church tower. Cross another wooden plank then keep straight on with the hedge on your left. Pause to enjoy the lovely countryside all around you.

8. A yellow arrow sign offers you a short cut to the village up the field but go straight on to a wide grassy track. There is a young woodland on your right. Look for a three storeyed farmhouse with a slate roof across the field.

9. Now comes a treat! A bank surrounds a beautiful reservoir where willow trees and clouds float in the smooth surface of the still water and where, as I passed, two white-face coots powered along leaving dark lines in their wake before one dived to re-emerge with something in his beak. Walk along the path that edges the water but go slowly and softly to savour the peace and beauty of this lovely spot. *(This is a perfect place for a picnic.)*

Pleshey countryside

Pleshey reservoir

You will come to *another* wooden bridge. Take a final look at the still water before you continue the walk. Now you're edging around a field, where a hollow tree is adorned with ivy. When you get to a concrete road turn right.

10. At a fork take the grassy track (left) between clipped hedges and fields, for this is the Essex Way. Climb gently to the road where the village hall appears to your right. This is a public bridleway. Cross the road (unless you wish to return to the village hall at this point) and follow the footpath to complete your exploration of the village.

When I walked here many wild flowers edged the pathway; clumps of pale primroses and clenched fists of cow parsley were just thinking about opening up to spring. By now I had been walking for about 1½ hours.

11. There are footpaths offering short cuts but carry on until you come to a road where you turn right. Here you will pass cottages, one with a greenhouse needing a few more panes of glass! You reach Vicarage Road as you enter the village and pass the earlier route you took to circle the earthworks. Continue along the road to reach a signpost. Turn towards High Easter (Back Lane).

12. Pass a building, possibly the old school, before you reach The Street where you turn right. The road gently slopes by pretty cottages and a curved house called Cobblers on your right. You will soon see The Leather Bottle a grade II listed building. The single storey part is 15th century.

   I called in to learn that the pub only re-opened two days before with a new landlord, Robert Reilly. He told me of plans to serve food once the kitchen had been cleaned from top to bottom. I wished him well.

13. A little further is Pleshey Mount viewing garden. There are benches to relax upon and watch wildlife in and around the moat where willows trail their leaves. The castle mound rises up – a tangle of undergrowth. An information board adds to the interest.

   Two Canada geese waddled across the grass and slid into the water when I stopped here.

14. Continue along The Street looking out for the other shop – The Old Stores that closed some years ago. The House of Retreat soon appears on your left. The sign says, 'Visitors Welcome.'

I went to the Reception and rang a doorbell. A lady took me along a passage to the garden and chapel. "Stay as long as you like," she said. The entrance was candle-lit. Inside the chapel it was serene and silent. I sat on a soft blue chair with a carpet beneath my feet and soaked up the stillness. Clear arched windows allowed in plenty of light.

Outside a brick path edged the herbaceous border full of many flowers. Tubs of pink and red tulips added colour; sweetly scented shrubs and a huge lilac tree enhanced the beauty.

My final steps took me past the still locked church and back to my starting place.

Walk 20: Greenstead Green

This circular walk offers scenic views as it takes you up and down through ancient woodland and along narrow lanes. It passes isolated farmsteads and returns you to the village where refreshments are available at Greenstead Farm.

Distance	4 miles or 6.4km
Time	1½ hours
Start	Greenstead Farm car park
Terrain	Up and down, steep in places
Map	OS Explorer 195 Braintree & Saffron Walden
Refreshments	In the barn is Hyacinth Tea Room open every day from 9am-4pm. 01787 476000. Booking is advised. There is a sunny bench in the clearing beside the woodland – a good place for picnic
Toilets	Greenstead Farm Café
Getting there	By narrow lanes not far from the A1124 and the A131 or the A120 through Stisted. Two miles south of Halstead. There are no regular buses and no train

I visited Greenstead Green in early spring and yes, there is a central green, with an old pump and spreading oak tree. There's the usual post box and village sign and a sunlit bench too. This is an unassuming little village with an assortment of houses both old and new lining the street. There are pretty flint cottages and the odd clue to the past, if you keep your eyes open.

1. Leave your car by the huge weather-boarded barn at Greenstead Farm shop where there is plenty of space to park. This is a good place both to start and end this walk - at the café within.

   Walk back to the road turning right at the gateway and a few steps takes you to the village green complete with sign, pump and bench. Here you can see The Old Post Office and Forge Cottages.

2. Opposite you can just make out the words 'Hare and Hounds' in the big bay-windowed house.

Old Post Office, Greenstead Green

I have childhood memories of Greenstead Green. Fifty years ago my father used to bring me here as a small child to buy apples from the little old man and little old lady – the Osbornes, who ran the post office with its sweet shop. Their sitting room with sweet smell of baking apples foil-wrapped in the Rayburn; friendly, floppy-eared spaniels and the treat that every child dreams of – choosing anything I wanted from the stacked shelves behind the counter, when Turkish Delight in a shiny purple wrapper – became my treasure. Once the little old man with watery, weary eyes picked a white rose and solemnly handed it to me. I've never forgotten. Now here I am again. The time for reverie over.

Set off past the village hall (with its ornate brickwork) and down the hill. You will see the buttressed walls of The Grange on your right. The road falls quite steeply here. There is a paddock to your left. You are approaching the brook and a small bridge, a good place to pause before you begin the uphill slope.

By the bank a white, hunched-up egret suddenly moved, stabbing at something in the soggy grass and a startled pheasant took off to make a low, whirring flight away from my unwelcome intrusion. The rain has galvanised the stream – it surged beneath the bridge, dragging at overhanging brambles.

3. The narrow road climbs past the greenhouses of Bourne Brook Nursery, then it's out into open countryside where fields fall and rise with the land the wind rattles last year's dry oak leaves.

4. At the top of the hill, where the road bends right at Claverings Farm (there are holiday lets here), there is the first good view of the village across the rolling fields. The spire of the church stands tall on the horizon.

5. Along this stretch of flat road you can see for miles!

Greenstead Green

1. Park at Greenstead Farm Shop near Village Green
2. Hare and Hounds
3. Bourne Brook Nursery
4. Claverings Farm
5. Views
6. Woodstack Corner
7. Moat Farm
8. Farmyard
9. Gladfen Hall
10. Wards Farm
11. Ravens Hall
12. Greenstead Farm Shop

View to the church

> *Here the road is lined with hedges, bearing evidence of the season; shrivelled blackberries and round, yellow leaves clinging to the hazel boughs where tiny catkins are forming. The bright-eyed face of a weasel appears, then a rustle in the grass and he is gone.*

6. Keep on the fairly busy road until you reach Woodstack Corner and the Nature Reserve – run by Essex Wildlife Trust. Here you follow the path to an information board about the flora and fauna. Keep watch for some of the creatures who live here. You are entering ancient woodland.

> *I always feel I must move gently and quietly if I am to see the creatures that live here. I lower my voice or simply walk in silence.*

The paths passed mossy banks. There are ponds and a choice of pathways, which all take you to the other side of the reserve. There is evidence of coppicing. You can bear left to follow the boundary fence passing over a wooden footbridge or you can stay on the bridle path but this way is much used by horses so it can be very muddy and walking can be difficult. Soon you will see a field to your right, follow the bridle path to a five-barred gate and a kissing gate that takes you back onto the hard surface of the road.

Bear right. Look for a thatched house, Mott Cottage which has two pheasants on the roof. The road winds its way around fields, woodland and from one isolated farmstead to another.

The author in the woods

My shadow accompanied me as the winter sun appeared to brighten the day. Across the field I glimpsed the spire of the church poking into the sky. Gosh, the village did seem far away!

7. Moat Farm stands all alone amidst trees with ivy twisted around them. I think it must be a lovely place to live. Hens wander freely by the gate.

8. Further along you come to a farmyard where chickens of many colours and sizes scrap for seeds. Iron pig troughs hold rain water and old pallets are stacked haphazardly.

   A big white cockerel crows from his perch on a post and a grey Silkie hen squawks in panic when I stop to peer over the gate.

At a junction ignore a left turn and bear right – towards Greenstead Green.

The brown blur of a sparrow hawk darted along the hedgerow. A sign pointed to the farm café. Now there's a spur to reach the village!

9. You pass some farm cottages then come to Gladfen Hall – a graceful old house, partly obscured by trees.

10. Wards Farm is next – much changed from the day my grandfather worked there as a horseman.

My father tells the story of a traction engine chugging up the drive and how its sparks set a leafy tree on fire! My grandmother used to take her three young children down this road to the village school every day – and push the heavy pram with the baby back! As I walk I try to picture her. My own legs are aching. How hard that must've been.

Take a final look at the views of open countryside for now the road falls away, down and down and soon you cross the fast-flowing stream again – then climb the next very steep hill.

11. At last you come to another rambling old farmhouse – Ravens Hall, with huge chimneys.

Mr Frost is in the garden – he has lived there all his life. He remembers his grandfather – a tenant farmer, buying it from Stisted Hall – it has been in his family ever since. The original house dates about 1500, but rooms have been added here and there over time, hence the quirky tiled roofs at different angles. In the garden is a pond surrounded by flowers.

Now as houses appear you are almost back to the village green *and* the farm café. Turn left at the crossroads and left again by the barns.

12. Greenstead Farm Shop is owned by Chris and Tania Butler. Chris's grandfather was Rab Butler – a politican who became Deputy Prime Minister. His son Sir Richard was president of the NFU and sought to protect incomes for farmers and farm workers during turbulent times.

Inside the huge 17th century thatched barn cartwheels dangled from the massive beams above. I sipped my hot chocolate and perused the menu.

'Game Terrine.' served with granary paddle or Soup of the day – Broccoli and Stilton. Hmmm! Just what I needed! I read that the food is locally sourced (many vegetables home grown) and they offer seasonal recipes, light lunches or coffee and cake. Sunday roasts or afternoon cream teas are also on offer. Outside a sheltered garden is a good place to eat on sunnier days.

Later in the gift shop I found local honey and preserves. There are candles and cards, mugs, place-mats and the Post Office. A short walk, turning left at the gate takes you by flint cottages to the church of St James that you saw across the fields, if you'd like to explore the village further. It should be open during daylight hours.

Greenstead Green cottages

Walk 21: Abberton

This walk starts and ends at Abberton Reservoir, a site of Special Scientific Interest carefully managed for conservation by Essex Wildlife Trust with Essex and Suffolk Water.

Constructed in the 1930s, it supplies much of Essex with drinking water. In 2013 it was enlarged and now stores 41 million litres.

There are reed beds, scrubland, grazing meadows, ponds and woodland providing valuable habitat for birds, mammals and invertebrates. Dragonflies, skylarks, water-voles and barn owls live here and nightingales sing in spring. There are nature trails, a gift shop, tea room and bird hides. It is open daily from 9am to 5pm. except for Christmas Day and Boxing Day. Donations welcome. In winter (when it closes at 4 pm), thousands of migrating birds stop over here on their journeys. There are special organised events. See www.essexwt.org.uk for details.

Distance	4.2 miles or 6.8km
Time	2½ hours
Start	Nature Reserve and Visitor Centre. Six miles south-west of Colchester. Postcode: CO2 0EU
Terrain	Mainly flat but gentle rises and falls in places
Map	OS Explorer 184 Colchester, Harwich & Clacton
Refreshments	Hare and Hounds. Layer Breton, serve lunch and evening meals. 01206 988757. info@thehareandhounds.net Closed Mondays. Booking advised. Abberton Reservoir Nature Reserve. 01206 738172 abbertonessexwt.org.uk Open every day except Tuesday. A good place for picnics
Toilets	As above
Getting there	By car: From Colchester take the B1026 through Layer de la Haye then onto the Reservoir. The Nature Reserve is clearly marked and soon appears on your left. By bus: First Essex runs the 175 and 67 service three times a day

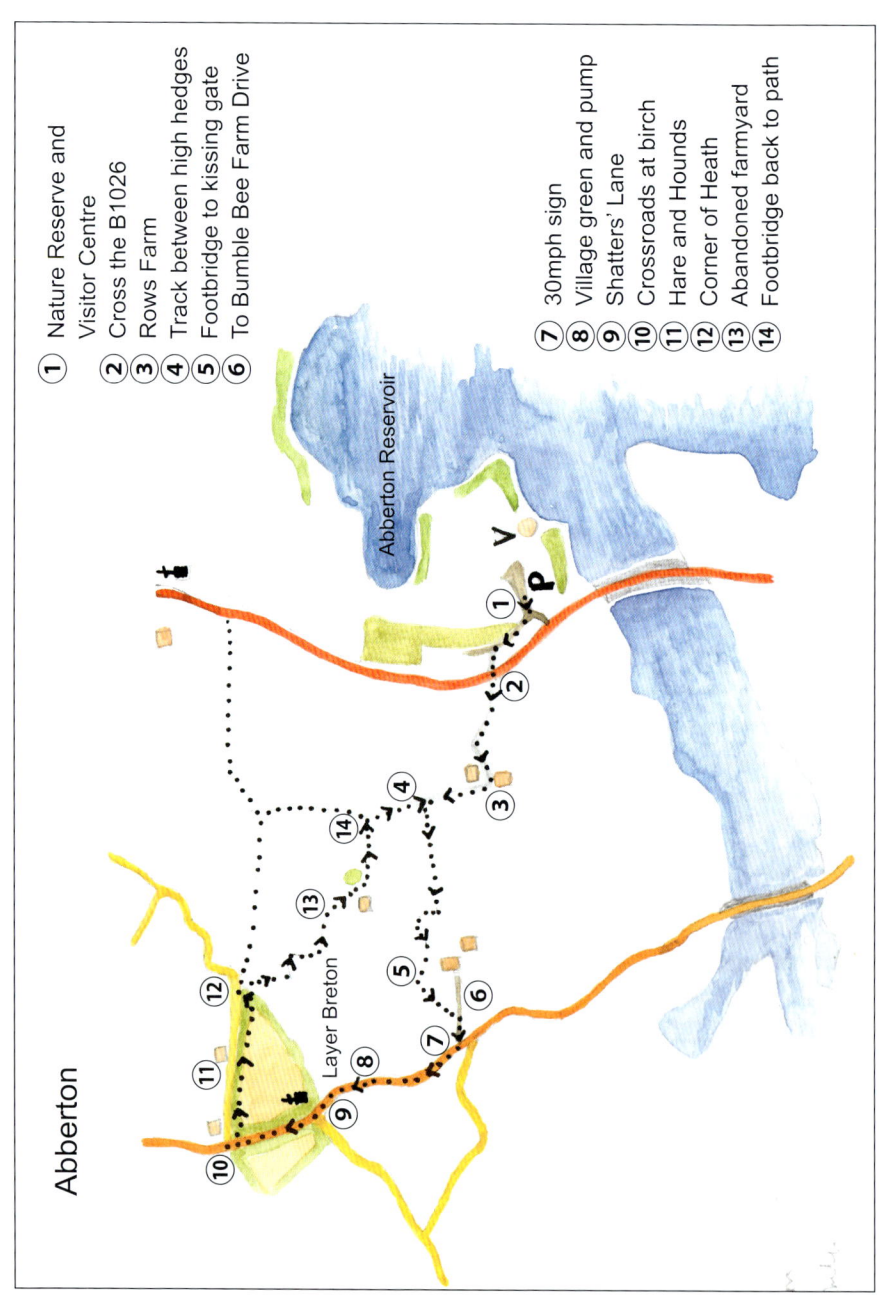

1. Follow the signs to the free Visitor Centre car park.

   I leave my car in a bay edged with beautiful wild flowers; fleabane, daisies, trefoil, purple knapweed and many I do not recognise. A stretch of blue water to my left sparkles in bright sunlight; so this is Abberton Reservoir. What a wonderful spot on such a sunny morning!

   Walk away from the Visitor Centre and turn right onto the old road to find a permissive footpath bordered by a hedge of elders draped with dog roses in summer.

   Beautiful wild flowers

   Turn left (towards the road) and follow a track on your right that runs parallel with the road.

2. The footpath crosses the road away towards Rows Farm where a sign points into the gently rolling Essex countryside of barley fields and brown butterflies. Behind you is a stretch of blue water and pylons tall against the sky.

   The narrow track edged with pink bindweed tangled in seeding grasses, climbs steadily upwards to the open sky.

3. Look for old weather-boarded barns and the buttressed brick wall of the farmyard as you scrunch across the loose gravel. Stop at the gate to turn back to enjoy the lovely view.

Farm road

Abberton view

A notice warns you that the buildings are dangerous, so no access. Then an arrow directs you right – across the old farmyard.

Huge white bindweed tumbles between brambles and creeps up over the barn roofs. The grassy track is dotted with white clover and edging the path goose grass fights for space with overgrown nettles. On my right the reservoir creates another lovely picture.

4. The track goes between poplar trees and high hedges. It becomes rutted. Turn left over a footbridge into a field. The path is clearly marked.

When I walked here the barley was just beginning to ripen into a soft pale gold.

You are heading to Layer Breton. In the distance is a brick church tower. Look for a yellow arrow by an oak tree when you reach the hedge line. Then enter another field and keep going to find another yellow arrow where you turn left over a wobbly footbridge that crosses a ditch.

5. Keep to the field edges, even if the path seems overgrown in places until you come to a kissing gate and another wooden footbridge. Now you walk

diagonally across a pasture of seeding grasses, vibrant with insects on a sunny morning. Ahead is a house, some horse chestnut trees and a wooden fence.

6. Here is Bumble Bee Farm and a grey house – Shalom Hall, with a collection of farm buildings.

An unseen screechy cockerel made his presence very clear.

7. Turn right passing red brick cottages and you will come to a road with a deep ditch on your right. At the sign post turn right to go up the hill to Layer Breton. The 30 mph sign tells you to take care – it's busy here. Walk on the grass verge. Houses, bungalows and cottages soon appear as you wander through the village.

8. Look for the village sign as you reach the highest point and the green with a rusty old pump. Across the road is the Old Post Office with pan-tiled roof and white weather-boarded walls. In summer the garden is full of roses. Beyond an iron gate is Breton Lodge before you come to Meadowside Cottage.

9. When you see Shatters Road on you left you are nearing St Mary's Church.

Near Birch

When I tried the door it was locked.

Now the scenery changes again as you enter heathland where willow herb flourishes. There is mixed woodland on either side with spindly silver birch trees. *The air is full of bird song.*

10. At the crossroads turn right towards Abberton and Layer de la

The Hare and Hounds, Layer Breton

Haye. The path creeps along the edge of the heathland. Over the road you will see a pub called The Hare and Hounds with benches outside and pretty hanging baskets.

If you need a comfort stop – this is a good place. They offer food during lunch hours and evenings.

11. Walk parallel to road beside the thick gorse bushes with the rough heathland on your right.

    Bright sulphur-yellow ragwort and plantain grow wildly amidst the tall, drying grasses where the vibrating sound of crickets indicate that summer is well underway. Cat's ear daisies are draped with tiny cobwebs.

    Across the road is the Old Chapel – now a private home. Another house sells country garden flowers – in the drive pretty bouquets are for sale.

12. You reach the corner of the heath and a gateway. Here is a choice of two footpaths. Turn right by an old iron-gate and squeeze round the post – with the hedge before you to your left. There are deep tractor tyre ruts.

13. Follow the track around the edge of the field until you walk right into an old abandoned farmyard of old abandoned outhouses, a derelict open sided barn beneath a rusty tin roof and the inevitable sea of nettles!

I felt a sense of deep sadness standing in this once cherished place, now so forgotten and desolate and I wondered what happened here to cause such neglect.

Look for a footpath sign by a gap in the hedges to your left that takes you away from the farmyard and across a field. *(It's easy to miss this one)*. It brings you to small copse and another field. Cross another wooden footbridge at the ditch and keeping the hedge to your left and the field to your right, follow the track. You will see the reservoir again ahead of you in the valley.

14. Turn right onto a wider track where the walking becomes easier and you will soon begin to recognise the route you travelled along earlier as we rejoin the footpath and retrace our steps to Rows Farm. Now the path drops down to the B1026 road. Cross again and bear right to return to the Visitor Centre. There is plenty to see here with boards and displays full of interesting information. You can also buy snacks and tasty cakes to enjoy as you sit on the terrace and look out over the water and reed beds, alive with wildlife.

If you have enough energy left – allow time to explore the reserve's footpaths and bird hides, follow nature-trail bridleways and linger at one of several viewing points. Listen for skylarks and watch for barn owls, cormorants and acrobatic terns. There are guided walks available at times so check the notice board to find out what's on offer.

Walk 22: Ulting

One of my favourite walks of all. Exploring farmland before dropping down to the canal/river for a stroll along the tow path then returning along narrow country lanes to my starting place and ending with a visit to All Saints church perched on the river bank.

Distance	4.3 miles or 7km
Time	2½ hours
Start	Park in Ulting. There are lay-bys near the School House
Terrain	Mainly level walking
Map	OS Explorer 183 Chelmsford & The Rodings
Refreshments	Duke of Wellington. 01245380246. Open every day from 11.00. Does take-aways. Hoe Mill is a good place for a picnic as is All Saints Church with a bench overlooking the river
Toilets	No public loos. The pubs offer comfort stops
Getting there	From the A12 find Hatfield Peverel near Witham and take the B1019 to Maldon. Look for a left hand turning to Ulting just as you leave the village. Drive about two miles. No buses

1. Park near to the Old School House and the village sign. (There's a convenient lay-by near the post box.) Walk away from the church (down its little lane) and along the road which might be busy, so take care – there is no pavement. Pass Brockley Cottages on your right and the Old Vicarage on your left. Then on a bend turn left onto a track.

2. Duck under a gate and walk a few steps before you turn right onto the footpath we are taking. It cuts straight across a field. A yellow arrow sign confirms the way.

The dark green spears of wheat were knee-high as I marched across the field towards the far trees. Two geese flew overhead – their necks outstretched. I could hear the distant roar of traffic from the A12. The sun was warm. I reached an oak tree whose leaves danced in the playful wind.

3. Bear left with the curve of the field – a yellow arrow points the route but at another oak tree keep to the field edge with woodland on your right. There is slight incline here. Soon you should see a fishing lake ahead. Pause to look back at the pretty view. A sign says; 'Members Only'. Turn right with the lake on your left then turn right again to reach a new field. Take care – stinging nettles grow well here.

4. Now bearing right follow the field edge beside woodland where brambles promise blackberries in months to come.

The field was a sea of seeding grasses. A kestrel hovered as if suspended on a string. A meadow brown butterfly fluttered across my path and from the hawthorn branches white blossom fell as confetti. An unseen wren sang – his whirring notes ending his song.

Field views

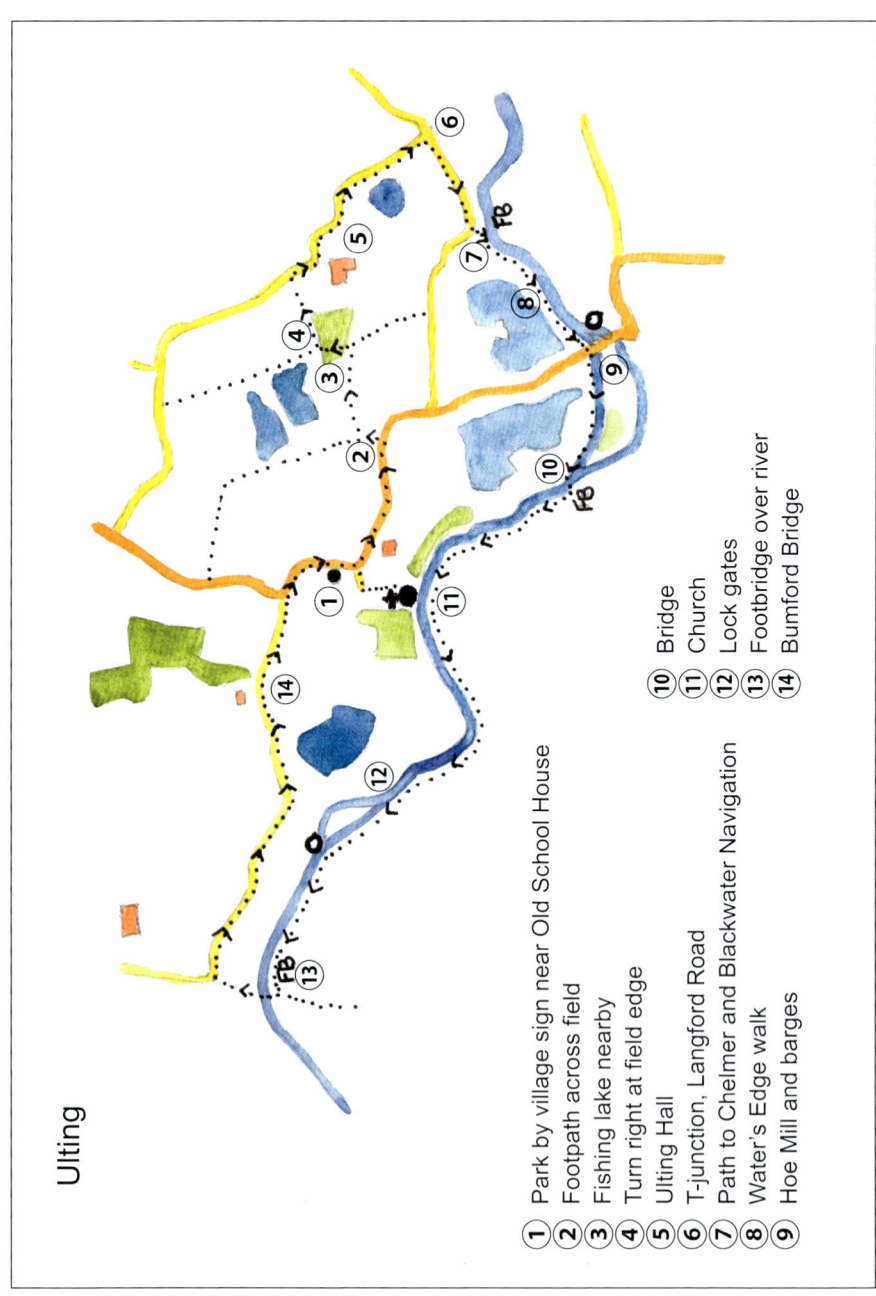

5. Soon you will reach a gate. Here is Ulting Hall Road. In the 16th century, this was a manor house. Today its barns and grounds are immaculate. You can get glimpses of the smooth lawn through the hedge. White gates appear on the right as the road curves left and the hall itself is partially visible.

A horse chestnut tree was in full flower, its white candlestick blooms dotted with dark pink. More pink could be seen in the pretty red campions. (I always knew them as 'plum-puddings' as a child.) The hedges created a shadowy world, painting stripes across the tarmac road.

6. At a T-junction turn right into Langford road.

7. Keep going until you see an old caravan and assorted junk, including stacks of wood, and turn left here by a gate post. There is no arrow but walk past a shed with a broken roof. In a few moments you will find yourself by the Chelmer and Blackwater Navigation (to give it the correct title). Turn right to begin a beautiful stretch of this walk by the water's edge. You are treading on the old tow path where as late as the 1960s

Ulting river

strong horses pulled barges carrying up to 25 tons of coal, bricks, timber or grain. Watch out for fish; tench, perch and pike skim along beneath the surface and sometimes jump to catch a fly.

The navigation of 13¾ miles was constructed to link Chelmsford to Maldon and the sea. It has 12 locks and 6 bridges.

8. Walk between back gardens and the ever-moving water. Enjoy the moment. You will reach a little wooden bridge with iron railings that takes you over a rush-filled ditch.

In one garden old forks stuck into the vegetable plots where asparagus grew. In the next was a paddling pool, a tree house and a barbecue ready for summer days. A great splash came from the river and I saw a big brown fish disappearing beneath the surface where lily pads floated like huge green plates. There were clouds of midges. A man was busy, trimming back the new growth along the path. He paused to talk, glad of a rest. He said Sugar Baker cottages were all that remained of a once thriving coal yard and the first sugar beet works in the country. I found out later that in 1832 Robert and James Marriage sought to reduce slave labour on the sugar plantations. They thought that if local beet was used there'd be less imported cane sugar. Thirty men and women were employed, but the cheap imports continued and the factory closed.

Look for a yellow arrow sign sending you straight on. A disused quarry on the right now serves as private fishery. There is another bridge ahead.

9. Here the river forks to create a canal. You have reached Hoe Mill. Cross the road to Hoe Mill Lock where there is a caravan site. A corn mill stood here until 1914. In the 1830s Hugh Constable, (with a famous artist for a brother) lived at Hoe Mill. Bear right beyond the bridge to follow the footpath sign. This is a pretty spot with moored barges and boats. There are benches and picnic tables if you need a rest. Take time to read the information board too.

I stopped for a photo or two, enjoying the peaceful scene of brightly painted barges, their reflections rippling in the water. Two mallards paddled along creating 'V' lines in their wake. From rushes a moorhen trilled. I read that in 1797 there were twelve locks and six bridges along this stretch of water.

Barges

The walk now takes you between the canal and the river.

I passed more boats and barges; 'Hobbit', 'Wild Goose', 'Isabella' and 'Bittern'. Some had tubs of flowers, others folded down parasols. Tall nettles grew on my left beneath willow trees where the wind whistled. I heard the roar of water, I had reached the weir.

10. At the weir where the river again joins the canal there is a little bridge. Keep following the river bank. There are more willow trees (planted for cricket bats) and farmland to your left until you come to woodland.

Buttercups shone yellow-gold amongst white comfrey. Under a trailing willow tree a swan curved her neck to probe the shallow water for tasty morsels. Another big fish caused a splash and a line of bubbles betrayed his presence. A robin sang – tremoring notes shrill in the quietness.

11. Soon you will see a tiny church built of flint, pebbles and brick on the far bank. There are 13th century arched lancet windows and a tiled spire points to the sky. This is All Saints. It dates from 1150AD. There is

evidence of an even earlier building on the site. In 1873 the church was falling down and had to be rebuilt and restored. At the end of the walk you can visit it, if you're not too weary.

A boat slowly chugged past the ancient building, creating a lovely scene.

Keep following the river passing woodland on your left then curving between two gateposts.

A meadow of seeding grass trembled in the wind and horses came to drink on the far bank. There were more willow trees then came the sound of a weir.

12. The river divides with the noisy weir on the right and lock gates ahead. Water is trickling from the closed gates of Rushes Lock. This is another lovely spot, a place to linger. There is a date 1926 and the maker was Maldon Iron Works Co. Ltd.

13. Continue your journey to a bridge spanning the river. There are high steps to access it and a bar to climb over. Once on the other side it's time to say goodbye to the navigation for here you must cross the field and find the little road – Bumford Lane that takes you back to your car. Turn right. You will see Cardfields Farm on your left beyond the sweep of field.

14. You will cross the stream at Bumford Bridge. The trees create a tunnel in summer. You pass several houses until you come to the busy road. Here

The ancient church

turn right. Look for The Owls, where terriers yapped furiously as I walked past. You'll soon be back to the start.

Before I leave I take the narrow lane to the ancient church. In dry weather 'parch marks' appear in the churchyard suggesting earlier structures. The north wall has Puddingstones – a conglomerate of dark brown pebbles. There are narrow lancet windows dated 13th century. Although the door is kept locked it is a peaceful spot with a bench – and would make a good place for a picnic or a well-earned rest.

Walk 23: Great Bardfield

I noticed several different weather-vanes on this route, you may enjoy finding them too as well as some I may have missed.

Distance	4.3 miles or 7km
Time	2 hours
Start	Roadside parking in Brook Street (or nearby) look for butchers shop or Memorial Cross
Terrain	Ups and downs – in places steeply so
Map	OS Explorer 195 Braintree & Saffron Walden
Refreshments	The Vine. 01371811822 info@thevinegreatbardfield.co.uk serves lunch and evening meals Wed - Sun, also take-aways. Between the Lines Bookshop. 0371810087 betweenthelines@gmail.com Open daily 10am-3pm
Toilets	In the above places
Getting there	The B1057 from Haverhill to Great Dunmow runs though Great Bardfield or from Braintree take the B1053 towards Saffron Walden and turn left to follow the signposts. Buses: Stephenson's 9A – one a day, Monday to Friday. Number 16. Chelmsford to Wethersfield four a day. Check times

1. *A circular walk out of the village to Waltham Cross then across fields passing a site of a watermill before returning to Great Bardfield where there are several places to visit. Some tricky stiles or barriers to negotiate!*

   Park your car on the roadside in the village. I find a spot outside Mr Smith's shop - the butcher with the award winning sausages. From here - or the Memorial Cross, set off down the hill of Brook Street towards a road junction to find the lane that leads to Waltham Cross (1 mile). Keep your eyes open for clues to the past. Look for The White Hart - once a retailer of wines, beers, spirits and tobacco.

2. Opposite the Co-op is Brook House where nearby water still trickles from the lion-headed pipe of the water fountain. This introduces us to the Smith family – so significant to the history of Great Bardfield. They were Quakers and gave the village its water fountain in 1860, the year after they built the Town Hall.

Great Bardfield village

As I stood by the flowing brook in the spring sunshine beneath trees laden with pink and white blossom, I spotted the nearby church tower and resolved to visit it later.

3. Cross the road, pausing to read the information board on Mill Green before you walk to Waltham Cross along Mill Road which climbs up and away from the village passing Gibraltor Windmill on the left.

The road to the windmill is private but you can admire it from afar. It was built in 1704 and could be the oldest one in Essex. It has an octagonal base

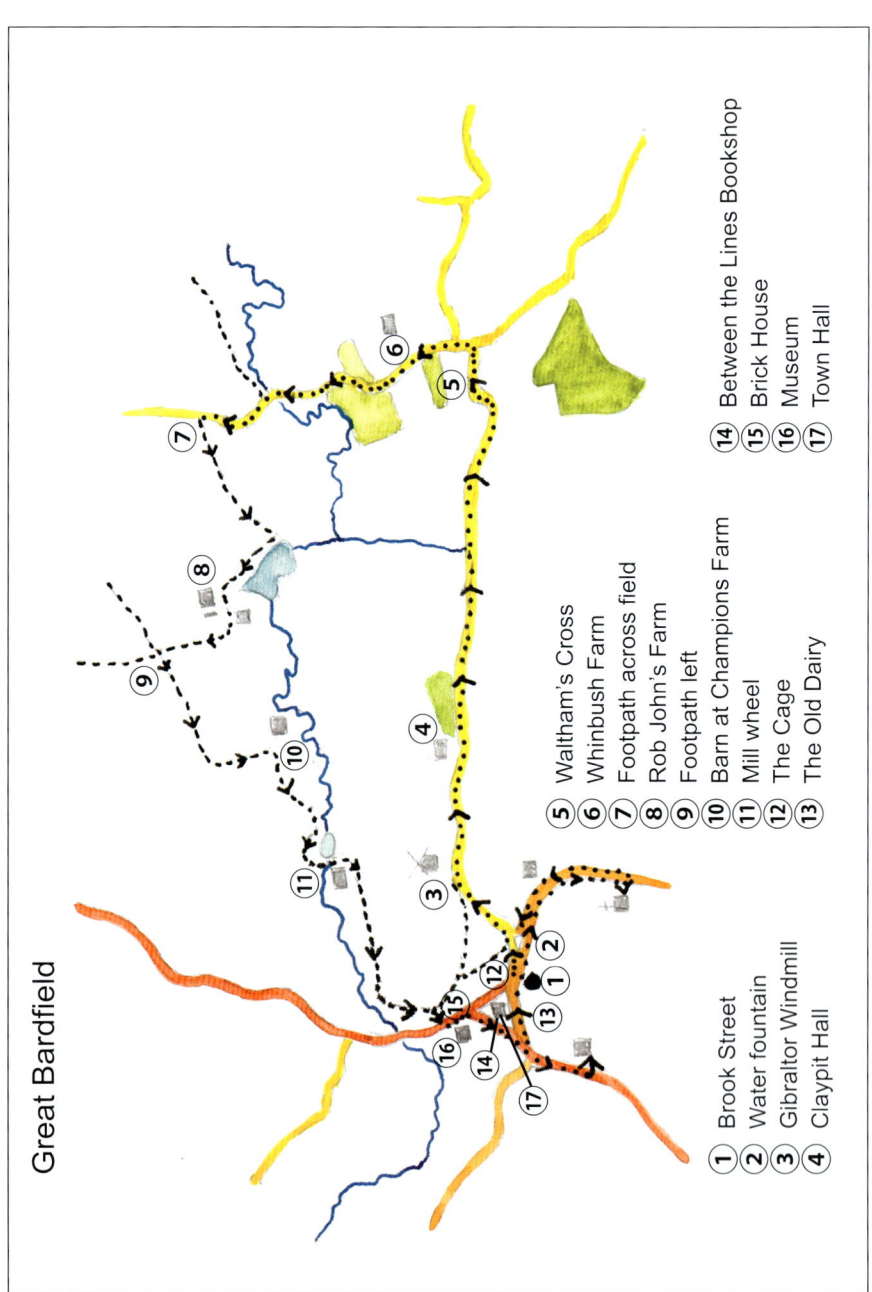

and an adjoining cottage – Gibraltor Cottage, for which there are deeds dating 1749.

In the 1840s the Smith family owned it and Thomas Samuel Dixon Smith worked the mill at night until his 87th year. This gentleman also wound up the church clock well into his 80s. It ceased milling in 1938 and became a private home in 1957.

Continue to climb the hill passing several pretty cottages with pan-tiled roofs as well as newer houses with neat gardens.

As I climbed higher passing Mill View, from behind the thick hedge on my left came the loud crow of a nearby cockerel. The steep bank brimmed with seeding grasses and an abundance of wild flowers including buttercups and cow parsley – still with tightly clenched white fists. Looking back I could see the windmill across the field, grey against the cloudy sky and there, faraway – the church. I buttoned my coat – for here the wind was fresh!

4. You will soon pass Claypit Hall where sheets billowed on the washing line. Look up to the barn roof where you'll see the weather-vane, can you tell which bird it features?

The road begins to fall between an orchard and a wheat field and it becomes more sheltered here. At School Farm (where I am told a head-teacher once lived) there is a brick wall around the farmyard and another animal on the weather vane. Can you find it?

The open views stretched for miles to a distant water-tower and dark shadows of clouds slid across the patchwork of fields edged with hedges.

You come to Hill Farm and then Orger's Farm partially hidden behind trees and shrubs. It is dated MCCCXX – and reminds me of a picture in a book of fairy-tales.

Here in Spring you will see bluebells by the roadside as you walk amongst trees that are full of birdsong. Soon you cross a stream.

5. Now you have reached Waltham's Cross, named after the crossroads. There are several pretty thatched cottages with delightful names such as Sweetbriar Cottage. Across the field on your right is a wood and here a

Bardfield countryside

stone coffin was found, now kept in the porch of the church I am told. At the cross roads turn left towards Finchingfield.

6. You will pass Chief's Farm where there is another bird upon a weathervane. Here is the warm smell of horses. The lane drops steeply between high hedges. Look for Whinbush Farm before you come to Sculpin's Bridge and the little River Pant flowing beneath the road.

Near to a pillbox on the right, a pool of water has attracted a gaggle of noisy geese both Canada and grey-lag and they protest as we pass. A squirrel dashes across the road. Many dark holes in the bank signal rabbits. After rain, this stretch may be full of puddles judging by the rutted, uneven surface.

7. Once across the bridge the road climbs out of the valley as it curves between oak trees. Look for a narrow path on the left that takes you straight across a big field.

The brown soil was ridged with lines as if a giant hand had drawn an enormous comb across it. The wind was chill but sunshine lit up the pretty landscape around me and in the distance I could still make out the windmill on the horizon.

8. When you reach the far hedge look for a stile and a footpath sign. You will also see a large pond, dotted with geese and ducks as you walk between a fence and hedge (beware nettles) turning right towards Rob John's Farm. The path takes you right into the farmyard, passing a stable block.

From within a stable came the sound of music, a radio was playing; someone was at work, the wheelbarrow and fork stood ready. Roberta the horse, stopped munching her mouthful of yellow hay to stare at me; the lake sparkled in morning sunlight; blossom was daubed in the trees. A lovely place to linger but I walked on, still with some distance to go.

The footpath leads beneath an arched hedge with a step down towards a timbered farmhouse. There are more buildings on the right. You pass a gateway and then turn right opposite a stable block to walk up a leg-achingly steep lane to enter open countryside again where you will be treated to more lovely views.

9. Where the lane curves right and another path tracks across the field before you, turn left to reach some trees where you'll find a broken stile to negotiate. *(It may be fixed by now.)* The path leads to the lower edge of a field, with the hedge on your left. When you see fences to paddocks turn left to walk between them towards Champion's Farm.

Great Bardfield Mill

10. By an old hanger/barn follow the grassy path with the hedge now on your right. It leads to a tiny footbridge over a brook and another broken stile. Then you come to *another* bridge where you turn right to walk by a wide

Mill wheel

field. Arrows confirm you are on track. You come to a five-barred gate and here is the site of the Watermill.

11. There is a rusty mill wheel where fast flowing water still noisily pours down between brick shafts. A willow trails its branches in the mill pond by the bridge. The lovely old mill house remains but alas, the mill was burned to the ground.

    I was told that there had been plans for Essex Heritage to take it over. Cheap imports had caused home-produced flour to dwindle and it had ceased to work. In 1993, locals recall seeing flames and someone driving away at speed. The son of the owner did not want other people there. He was tried for arson and received a prison sentence.

    With the house on your right look for an arrow that directs walkers along a grassy track between hedges. Soon you will hear the sound of traffic and see houses ahead. There is a deep drop to the stream on your right, so take care.

12. Follow the path to the right, over a footbridge to pass back gardens before reaching the street. Turn left and walk by a terrace of brick cottages back into Great Bardfield. Look out for The Cage, the 1816 lock-up for drunks and vagabonds. If it is open (weekends mainly) sit inside and listen to the old Essex voice telling its history and peer into the darkness to make out a shadowy figure.

13. Pass Cage Cottage where the artist Sheila Robinson lived. Turn right at North Place where you will see The Old Dairy. Long ago cows were herded along the street for their daily milking. In 1984 it became a private house.

14. The Vine offers food but look for 'Between The Lines' – the bookshop where you can enjoy coffee and conversation.

    Inside the bookshop I meet Jenny who bravely opened six years ago, and hasn't regretted it a minute. 'Books are back in fashion', she tells me. I enjoy a pot of tea and a slice of fruity flapjack before she directs me on to the Cottage Museum. Armed with an information sheet about the Bardfield Artists I set off up the hill. During the 1950s Bardfield became a centre for the arts. Local artists opened their homes and studios for two weeks of exhibitions.

15. As you walk along the main street look out for Brick House where Eric Ravilious and Edward Bawden (who created a series of lithographs about the English village) worked; Trinity Cottage where Marianne Straub designed textiles and Town House the home of the pacifist Kenneth Rowntree who contributed to the Recording Britain Project. Don't miss the signpost to Little Bardfield. It will bring a smile to your face!

16. Just beyond The Bell you will find a low thatched 16th century alms-house where Nellie Bright lived with no electricity or mains water until 1958. The Great Bardfield History Society restored it and it opened as a museum in 1961.

    Inside are fascinating exhibits of local crafts; information about local characters and a kind lady, Janet who is happy to answer my questions. Entry is free – but do make a donation.

17. Retrace your steps to the car. Close to the Memorial Cross is the 1804 Quaker Meeting House where I end my exploration of Great Bardfield. There is a quiet garden where passers-by can pause a moment and sit amidst the headstones of Joseph Quartius Smith, Matilda Rickman Smith, Sarah Smith and many others. Perhaps a good place to reflect on all you've discovered this afternoon?

Great Bardfield street

Walk 24: Beaumont cum Moze

This walk explores the coastal countryside edging the North Sea, not far from the busy seaside town of Walton on the Naze. Here are great stretches of mud flats with veins of tiny creeks reaching inland. One such is Landermere Creek and our walk includes its most westerly point – Beaumont Cut.

Distance	4.3 miles or 7.6km
Time	Up to 3 hours
Start	Brook-Lynne Farm Shop car park
Terrain	Steep upward incline in the final stages
Map	OS Explorer 184 Colchester, Harwich & Clacton
Refreshments	Fresh fruit in farm shop. Pubs in nearby Thorpe le Soken or for a treat, fish and chips in Walton. Landermere Creek is a wonderful place for a picnic
Toilets	None in Beaumont
Getting there	From the A120 take the A133 to Weeley then the B1033 to Thorpe le Soken. Turn left taking the Harwich road to Beaumont and Great Oakley. In Beaumont bear left to find Brook-Lynne Farm Shop. This is a good place to leave your car. There are no buses

1. Start at the well outside the barn, bright with red geraniums when we walked here. With Willow Cottage to your left, cross the road, and look for a footpath sign pointing towards Kiln Cottage. Here you walk by a gate which warns you of a strange dog!

   (To confirm his presence, the unseen strange dog barked furiously as we passed.)

   You come to a stile to your right. Follow the well-trodden path. A pond can be seen on your left with a sign; 'Deep Water'. Here is woodland one side and a field on the other.

2. When you come to a corner of the field drop down the bank and turn right to walk another field edge. Ferns grow on your right but in the fields the farmer grows vegetables, so far rhubarb and potatoes.

Beyond the seemingly endless lines of flowering potatoes, cottages could be seen among trees. A wind turbine spun frantically in the sea breeze.

You reach a footbridge on your right with a yellow arrow, cross the ditch, then almost immediately you see another footbridge that takes you left across the ditch again. This might be overgrown.

3. Now turn right and walk along this field.

The hedgerow was twined with wild roses and fragrant honeysuckle. Amongst tall seeding grasses stood taller thistles and cow mumble with swollen buds. In an old oak was an owl box. The footpath was half hidden in long, damp grass.

4. Where the field curves look for another footbridge onto the busy Harwich Road which you must cross at this point. The footpath continues with a garden fence on your right. On a gatepost is a picture of a horse – Bearland who died in 2017.

Now follow the grassy path behind outbuildings. It becomes narrow and overgrown. The hedge is to your left. Soon you come to trees where the path drops to a footbridge and brings you to another field.

We detoured to take the steps up the bank on our left to peep at the reservoir where swallows skimmed.

5. Go straight on with the field now on your right. Here you can see a distant view of the coast. Turn left at a yellow arrow under an oak tree and walk through woodland. A picnic bench is on your left. At another footbridge turn right and see a lovely vista of faraway fields. Bear right until you come to a crossroads of footpaths. Turn left to walk uphill through the field. There is a bungalow to your left, with a big conservatory and you will hear the sound of traffic.

6. Turn right just before you reach a house and walk down towards the sea. Keep beside the boundary hedge.

Beaumont view

This was a lovely stretch, the land falling away before us. The sun-baked track led beneath oak trees whose shadows painted stripes of dark green, indeed we seemed to be in a green landscape. Beneath our feet white clover and pink bindweed added colour.

7. You come to yellow arrow on your left, beneath an oak, which directs you right across the field before you in a slightly diagonally direction.

When we walked, oilseed rape stood higher than me and heavy with pods leaned over the path. It was a jungle to be waded through. Thankfully when we reached the hedge line and saw the footpath sign we knew we were on course.

At the hedge look for a yellow arrow and a stile. Go straight across the next field of rough pasture.

Horses grazed the sparse grass amidst the thistles, sedge and greater spearwort buttercups.

We climbed over a broken stile and then crossed a footbridge and went straight on.

After a stile you see a farm beyond a ditch to your right and an open field to your left where a pill box is visible as well as farms and tiny cars flashing by on the road. This is a wide track beside ash trees, and tall poplars can be seen ahead.

8. You come to Lower Barn farmyard where enterprising folk create handmade furniture and kitchens in the barns.

There was a joinery and from a forge came the sound of voices. In the farmyard was a lovely old barn with a tin roof; silent, empty pig styes and an old cart lodge where ivy scrambled. In a Nissen hut stood a tractor. The farmhouse stood beyond immaculate gardens. On the right appeared two telephone boxes, a red post box and half a landmine on a lawn. Outside a livery were bags of hay and the usual plastic buckets.

9. Cross the yard to a footpath sign by a dog poo bin. The path leads through a small copse and a few steps later you find yourself standing by

Landermere Creek

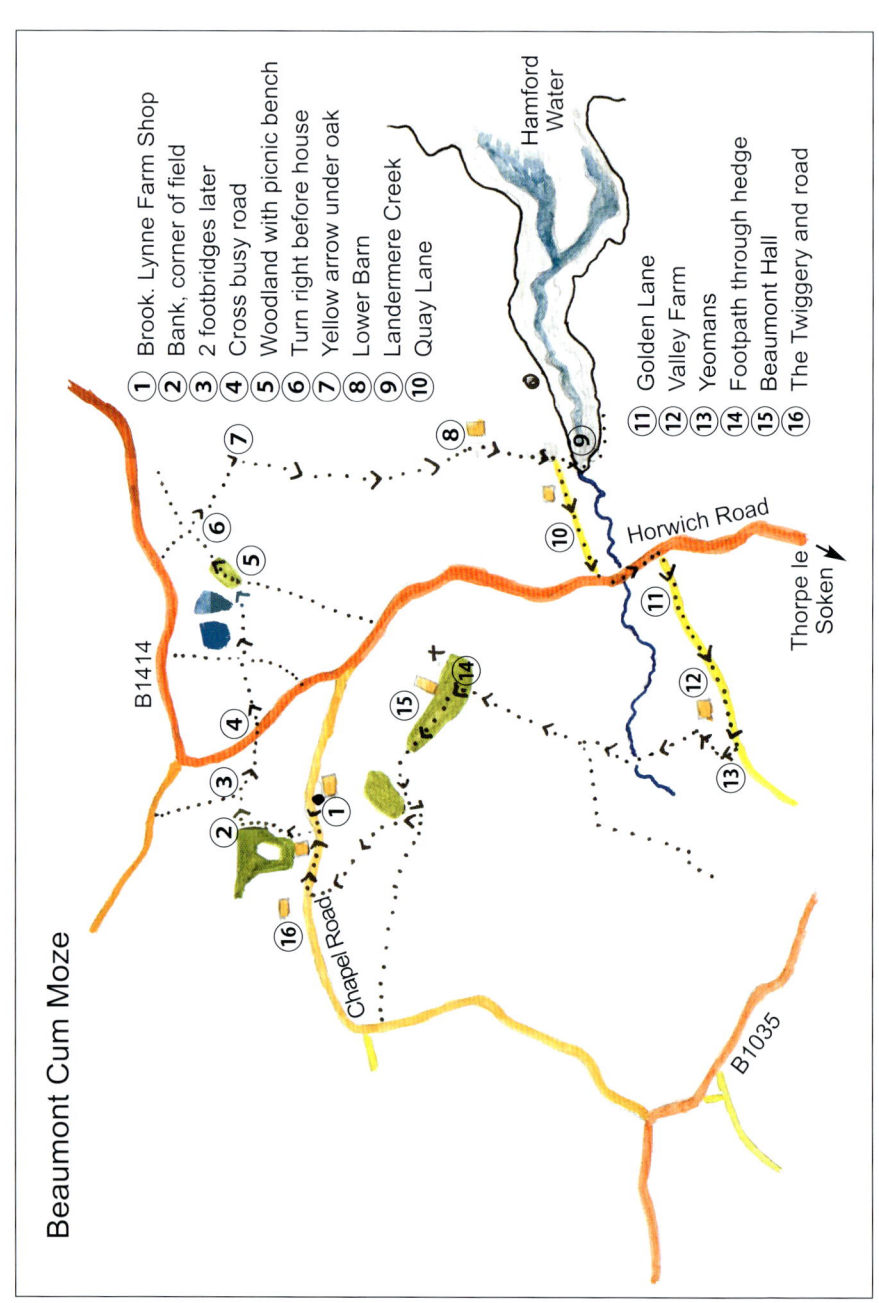

Landermere Creek. Suddenly you are surrounded by a wide open space of salt marshes and sky. You may wish to linger and explore here, as I did before you continue your walk.

In the mud below us was the skeletal form of an old boat, abandoned; quietly decaying. A black-headed gull squawked above our heads and a heron slowly flapped his big wings and lifted from the shallow water. I clambered down the steep bank in search of hidden treasure. My homework served me well. Beyond a small store building I found it. The mound of the brick kiln – a scheduled ancient monument and a link with days long ago. There were steps down to the arched doorway and into the darkness. Sunlight streamed down the open central chimney, and where once chalk had been burned at high temperatures to make lime, hollyhocks and foxgloves now grew. On the mound above purple mallow flowered alongside bristly ox-tongue, and clouds of hoary cress, altogether a lovely spot.

I discovered that this is a rare example of an East Anglian lime kiln. Lime was used for fertiliser, in food and to produce gas and oil. Thames barges such as 'Rose' the 42 ton barge, now the wreck you can see, took cargoes of food and grain to London and bought back night-soil to spread on the land. She was launched in 1880 and for fifty years worked this coastal route.

East Anglian lime kiln

There was a canal here in Roman times to link the land to Hamford Water and the North Sea. This final stretch is called the Beaumont Cut and was built in 1832 using stones from the old London Bridge, they are still there. It closed in the 1930s but small boats can still access it – as I saw on my return trip. I also read that the Beaumont Cut featured in 'Secret Water' – a novel written by the children's author, Arthur Ransome in 1939.

10. Retrace your steps to the farmyard and turn left to walk the lane passing Quay Farmhouse on your right. When you reach the end of Quay Lane at a busy road junction turn left.

11. Proceed with care – the verges offer some safety as cars whizz by. The road curves and then you see your turning – Golden Lane on the right.

12. This is a long straight, uneventful road – with an incline and high hedges – not an easy stretch on a hot day (as I discovered). You pass a house called Longshots Meadow before Valley Farm on your right.

13. Just beyond it the footpath (right) takes you down steps and through the hedge onto rough farmland. Bear right to walk towards the barns then turn left down a farm track. Now the hedge is to your left. The path drops to a stream then begins a long, steep uphill stretch by the side of a field.

14. Stick to this path, ignoring a footpath going left, until you come to woodland. There is a gateway and footpath sign under an ash tree.

The day was hot now with little breeze and we were glad to reach the shadows of the trees. A crimson Cinnabar moth fluttered across our path, at home amidst the yellow ragwort that flourishes here and the views were lovely but now my legs ached and I was too weary to really notice.

The church of St Leonard and St Mary

15. Soon the red bricks of Beaumont Hall appear on your right, where it peeps over the trees. Once beyond the woodland go straight across one field then bear right to skirt around the field edge. Look for a yellow arrow on your right that points you through the hedge-line and over a ditch.

16. Turn right to walk towards the village. There are farm buildings to your left. Nearly back now! As you meet the road opposite 'The Twiggery' turn right to return to the Farm Shop where you began.

You may wish to stop at the church of St Leonard and St Mary on your way to Thorpe le Soken where there are several eateries, or perhaps take the short drive into Walton to paddle in the sea.

The wreck of 'Rose'

Walk 25: Chappel and Wakes Colne

This is my longest walk but still not too demanding, exploring the rural landscape as it rises from the Colne Valley to the north east of Colchester. The feature of the railway with its museum adds extra interest along the way. The waiting room gives an insight into days long ago.

Distance	5 miles or 8km
Time	2¾ hours – and time to linger at the railway museum and café
Start	The East Anglian Railway Museum. Free parking spaces here
Terrain	Some steep places up and down as well as the steps over the footbridge
Map	OS Landranger 168 Colchester, Halstead & Maldon
Refreshments	The Chappel Station Café (free access) 01787 223381. ext. 246. info@platform2cafe.co.uk Serves food Fri- Sun 10-5. The Swan public house down by the river offers a more extensive menu. 01787 222353 www.swaninn-chappel.com
Toilets	The Railway Museum. The Swan
Getting there	By car: 8 miles from Colchester. CO6 2DS. Turn north from the A604 from Colchester to Halstead at Wakes Colne. A regular train service runs from Sudbury, Bures or Marks Tey where there is a connection to the main London line. There is disabled access to the platform – but you will need a car to access both sites of the museum. A 716 bus runs on school days. Check up to date times

1. Start by the Railway Museum where there is parking by a slip road. If you need some refreshment, or the toilets to set you up for this longer walk, pop into the museum first.

If not walk back towards the road and find a footpath on your right that runs parallel to the road itself by the side of a fenced field. As you look across the field you will see the goods shed, old rolling stock and station buildings including the Railway Tavern, once a pub called The Sunderland Arms. It closed in 1964.

The path takes an upward slope and is edged with burdock, red campion and stinging nettles.

2. You will come to the road where a signpost points you to Fordham. Turn right into a narrow lane that leads over the railway bridge. A sign tells us that if we witness a vehicle striking the bridge we must contact ... a telephone numbers follows.

As nothing as exciting as this is happening I content myself by

The author outside the Railway Museum

Chappel railway from bridge

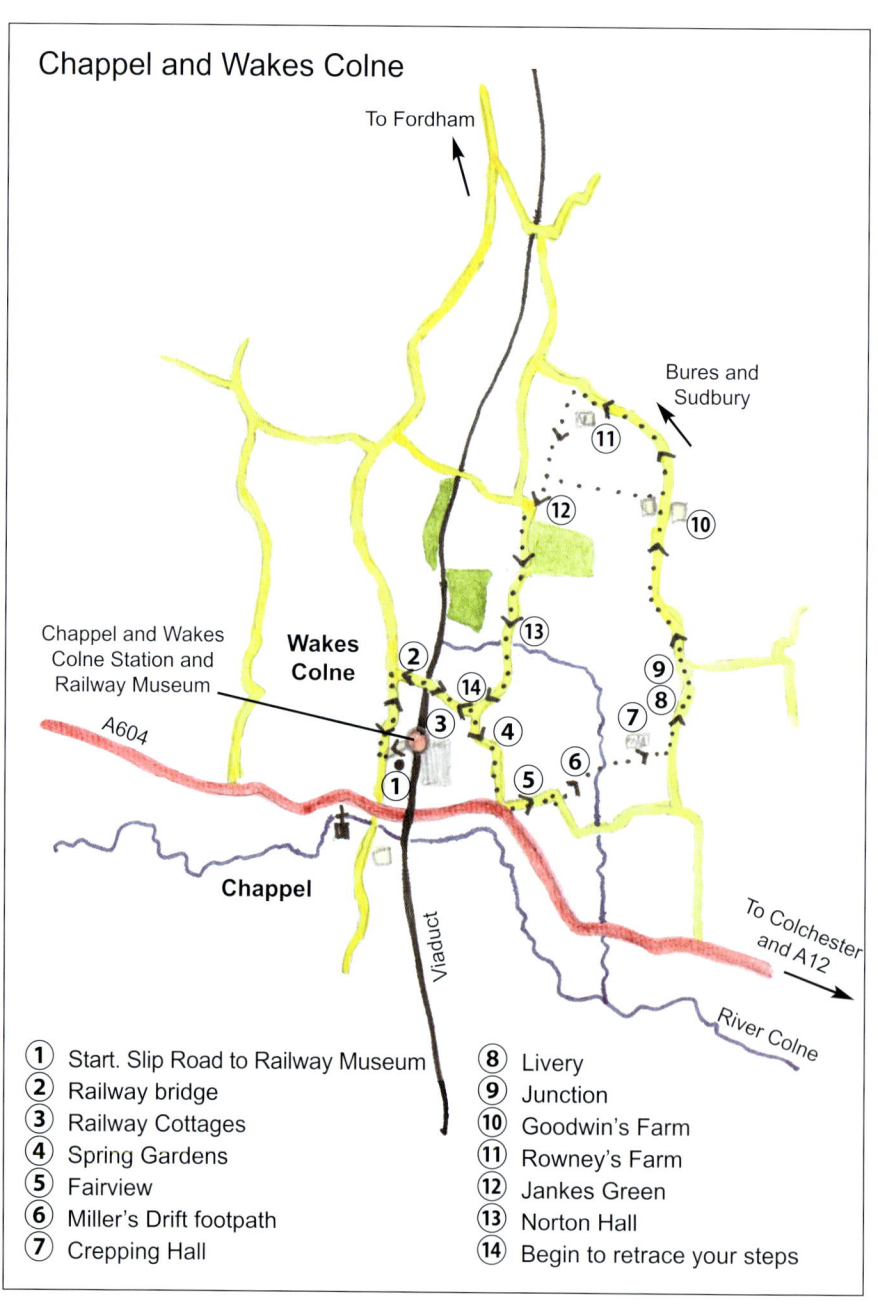

leaning on the bridge and gazing down the line. Beside me purple vetch curls up the seeding grasses and the white anthers of ribwort plantain form a ring around the rusty brown flower heads. Common vetch was once used for cattle fodder.

3. Continuing the walk you soon reach Railway Cottages where in summer unusual roses bloom in the garden of No. 1. Now you are entering open countryside with fields of silky barley when I walked this way.

4. When you come to a junction with a central triangle of grass, turn right to walk downhill. Hedges soon give way to trees then comes Spring Garden Road with slate-roofed cottages.

5. At a crossroads turn left by a pond as the road climbs steeply up and away from the sound of traffic. Look for Green Acres Farm on your right where caravans are welcome. A house inappropriately named 'Fairview' overlooks them through a thick hedge.

6. The road curves right before you see a footpath on your left. This is Miller's Drift Walk. Here you leave the road and step out through a grassy meadow keeping the hedge to your right. Look for alder trees with their smooth bark. You will see a footbridge and a yellow arrow sign which takes you through woodland before you climb again between some young saplings planted on either side.

As I walked here the sweet, warm smell of cut hay greeted me. I noticed the gathering clouds and hoped the rain would not come too soon. From a woodland ahead the piercing notes of a robin's song added to the beauty. Dog roses clambered in the hedges, their petals blushed with pink.

7. You reach a wooden gate on the left where the path leads beneath low branches of oak trees that edge the moated Crepping Hall which is partly visible.

Crepping Hall (Grade I listed) was built in the late 12th century. The arched oak doorway is dated 1314. It has been remodelled over the years. In 1349 it is recorded that thirteen tenants on the Crepping Hall estate died before the summer was out, probably of plague.

The path led across pastureland where strands of sheep's wool were snagged on the thistles. Sheep heavy with fleece, stared as I passed.

8. At the road turn left to pass barns and the livery. Keep to the road ignoring footpath signs that would take you across the fields.

9. You will come to a junction where a signpost leans precariously. Here you bear left towards Sudbury and Bures. Telegraph poles edge the road.

   A pigeon settles on the wires and above him gliders hang in the sky. A woman's voice can be heard; someone is calling instructions to riders on horses at Hemps Farm Livery.

10. Look for Goodwins Farm with its cream coloured painted bricks under a slate roof. A thick hedge screens the house from the road and curious passers-by. There are barns and outbuildings with cobwebbed windows. Along the verges here are many wild flowers. *Look for herb Robert with stripy pink petals and lobed leaves; yellow cat's ear on leafless stems with tiny brown bracts (giving the plant its name) and upright hedge parsley with delicate white flowers and leaves of fern-like fronds.*

    Another glider, a huge silent bird sweeps over the wheat field. You reach The Observatory with ornamental trees in the gardens.

Potatoes

From somewhere close at hand came the strident mewing call of an unseen peacock.

11. Next come the tumbledown barns and bungalow of Rowney's Farm.

    A pitchfork and shovel leaned against the door of the barn where wisps of straw littered the concrete. By an ancient waggon bearing painted 'FRUIT AND VEGET' on its side stood an assortment of plastic buckets, some brimming with brown potatoes.

    Here you leave the road by a gap in the hedge and cross a wooden footbridge into a field. Turn left for a short distance until you see another yellow arrow that points you left again back towards the farmyard with its assortment of tumbledown sheds, old tractors and rusting farming implements. Turn right to find an overgrown path between a pasture with a barbed wire fence and a hedge which hides long abandoned farm machinery.

    Cows lifted their heads to watch us and a startled peacock dashed for cover.

12. Soon you reach an open field with a central oak tree. Make a beeline for this then on to the other side and the hedge. Look for the yellow arrow. Then walk with the hedge on your right and a wood on your left until you come to a country road. This is Jankes Green. Turn left to follow the road. Soon it climbs to Norton Hall Farm.

13. You pass Holly Cottage before the road dips and comes to Norton Hall itself. The road continues to fall to the valley where by the stream a footpath on the right takes you around the field edge and back to the railway cottages. If it is muddy, keep going on the steep upward road which levels out at the junction you visited much earlier in the walk.

    I stopped to rest my aching legs and stared back at Norton Hall, the narrow lane edged with hedges and the gathering clouds.

14. Bear right at the junction to retrace your steps, past the Railway Cottages, over the bridge and back to the Railway Museum.

    I clambered up the steps and stood on the footbridge. On one side there was a signal box, painted green and cream, rolling stock and the goods shed

The viaduct

with arched windows. Far to the right was a children's play area and grassy meadow for picnics. Looking in the other direction revealed lovely views over the Colne valley with grey leaved willow trees beyond the rusty roofed carriages.

Down on the platform are notices about construction of the railway, which has remained virtually unaltered over the years. In the

The Street, Chappel

booking office is an iron fireplace where people huddled on cold mornings. The viaduct was built from 1847-49. In 1865 the line was extended from Sudbury to Cambridge and in 1914 renamed Chappel and Wakes Colne Railway. In 1963 Dr Beeching's report was published and the branch line marked for closure. In 1970 the Stour Valley railway preservation society moved onto the site.

I ended my visit here with a short drive down to the village. From the bridge and the garden of The Swan you get a good view of the viaduct. If you have time, wander past the old cottages and little school in this pretty, little place.

Also from Sigma Leisure:

Walks in the Slow Lanes of Suffolk
Angie Jones

Suffolk – a county of beautiful rolling farmland and narrow, winding lanes leading to sleepy villages and ancient wool towns with towering churches and forgotten castles.

This book invites you to explore twenty-five gentle walks. It is for the unhurried wanderer who likes to linger, those with an afternoon to spare and time to reflect over a cuppa and cake.

The walks explore tiny hamlets where humble cottages cluster around a country church built from hand-gathered flints or villages full of grand timber-framed houses – evidence of the prosperous woollen cloth trade; or walks that simply explore woodlands, fields and footpaths around isolated farmsteads.

Each walk has a hand painted map and pastel sketch as well as descriptive, personal recollections – all the work of the author, Angie Jones. There is also background information and local history, (sometimes from the mouths of people she meets along the way) to enhance the adventure and create a journey of discovery.

£12.99